Ancient Rhetoric and Oratory

BLACKWELL INTRODUCTIONS TO THE CLASSICAL WORLD

This series will provide concise introductions to classical culture in the broadest sense. Written by the most distinguished scholars in the field, these books survey key authors, periods, and topics for students and scholars alike.

Ancient Rhetoric and Oratory

Thomas Habinek

Blackwell
Publishing

BLACKWELL PUBLISHING
350 Main Street, Malden, MA 02148-5020, USA
108 Cowley Road, Oxford OX4 1JF, UK
550 Swanston Street, Carlton, Victoria 3053, Australia

First published 2005 by Blackwell Publishing Ltd

Library of Congress Cataloging-in-Publication Data

Habinek, Thomas N., 1953–
Ancient rhetoric and oratory / Thomas Habinek.
    p. cm. — (Blackwell introductions to the classical world)
    Includes bibliographical references and index.
    ISBN 0-631-23514-0 (alk. paper) — ISBN 0-631-23515-9 (pbk.: alk. paper)
    1. Rhetoric, Ancient. 2. Speeches, addresses, etc., Greek—History and criticism. 3. Speeches, addresses, etc., Latin—History and criticism. 4. Oratory, Ancient. I. Title. II. Series.
    PA181.H33 2004   2005
    808'.00938—dc22   2004005864

A catalogue record for this title is available from the British Library.

Set in 10.5/13pt Galliard
by Graphicraft Limited, Hong Kong
Printed and bound in the United Kingdom
by TJ International, Padstow, Cornwall

The publisher's policy is to use permanent paper from mills that operate a sustainable forestry policy, and which has been manufactured from pulp processed using acid-free and elementary chlorine-free practices. Furthermore, the publisher ensures that the text paper and cover board used have met acceptable environmental accreditation standards.

For further information on
Blackwell Publishing, visit our website:
www.blackwellpublishing.com

Contents

Preface

Oratory is formal public speechmaking. It is the characteristic political act of ancient city-states and of later political entities that draw their inspiration from them. Rhetoric is the study of available means of persuasion. It came into being as a distinct intellectual and social enterprise because of the prevalence of oratory in classical antiquity. Rhetoric analyzed successful instances of oratorical persuasion and derived from them principles that could be applied in new situations. Ancient legends concerning the origin of rhetoric date its commencement to the moment when tyranny ceased and collective deliberation began. Modern philology belittles such accounts, noting a gap of a century or so between the expulsion of the tyrants at Athens and the attestation of the word rhetoric in Greek. But ancient legend contains a truth deeper than philology: creation of and reflection on special speech go hand in hand; and oratory and rhetoric together constitute the special speech of the ancient state.

The ancient partnership of rhetoric and oratory is the topic of this book. Why did rhetoric and oratory matter to ancient societies? What do they offer to student, scholar, and citizen today? The subject is a vast one and can legitimately be approached from a number of perspectives. The perspective adopted here is primarily sociological. Our concern is to understand how rhetoric and oratory operated within the civic life of ancient Greece and Rome and, by implication, how they might come to operate in a revived civic culture today. This study will introduce the reader to important texts and writers in the history of rhetoric, to the most famous and influential orators, to the controversies sparked by the popularity of rhetoric, to key aspects and effects of rhetorical education, and to representative moments in the afterlife of classical rhetoric from late antiquity through the present. But the focus will be less on rhetoric as a system of verbal production and more on rhetoric and oratory as social practices; less on the history of a discipline or literary genre, and more on the political and social implications of rhetoric's ascendancy, decline, and revival. Comprehensiveness is out of the question. Instead, the inspiration for this book is the ancient genre of protreptic (Greek) or exhortation (Latin), which aimed to give the reader just enough information about a subject to whet the appetite for more. As the root *trep-* in Greek suggests, this protreptic aims to "turn" the reader in the direction of studying classical rhetoric.

Many who write on rhetoric – going back at least to Aristotle – apologize for their subject matter, presenting it as, in effect, "philosophy light," embarrassed that it complicates pure reason with emotions, interests, and, seemingly worst of all, embodied performance. They warn the reader not to take too seriously the negative connotations of the modern adjective "rhetorical," even as they reinforce that negativity. There are even contemporary political theorists who work valiantly to develop and defend what they consider to be non-rhetorical modes of discourse, styles of communication stripped of contingency, emotion, personal or group allegiance.

This book takes a different stance. It makes no apology for rhetoric and suggests you make none either. Rhetoric (and here, as often throughout this book, I use the single term "rhetoric" as shorthand for "rhetorical training and analysis together with oratorical performance"), whatever its challenges and limitations, is the discourse of citizens and subjects, in all their glorious specificity, struggling to recompose the world. It may be competitive or collaborative, celebratory or belittling, and, in time, written as well as spoken. It is alternately exclusive and inclusive, deceitful and illuminating. It often reinforces hierarchies, and just as often disrupts them. But it is always social, always interested in engaging the range of human faculties and the diversity of human experience, and always of the moment. Its disciplined yet unpredictable nature well suits the ancient view that the essence of political life is the willingness to govern and be governed in turn. Nietzsche put it well when he said of participation in rhetoric that "one must be accustomed to tolerating the most unusual opinions and points of view and even to taking a certain pleasure in their counterplay; one must be just as willing to listen as to speak; and as a listener one must be able more or less to appreciate the art being applied."[1] Art, argument, conviction, power, but also play, pleasure, tolerance, and exchange: these and more describe the experience of ancient rhetoric – and await its modern student as well.

I am happy to express my gratitude to Professor Carolyn Dewald and to Ross Faith of the USC Debate Team, both of whom read and commented on an earlier version of this book. Professor Dewald in particular saved me from a number of errors. In addition, I am grateful to Al Bertrand of Blackwell Publishing for his encouragement and advice throughout the composition of this book and to students who have enrolled in my courses on various aspects of ancient rhetoric and oratory, both at Berkeley and at the University of Southern California.

Chronological Chart

---

800 BC   Legendary date for founding of Rome by Romulus and
Remus, 753 BC
Composition of *Iliad* and *Odyssey*, approx. 750 BC
Composition of Hesiod's *Theogony*, approx. 730 BC

700 BC   Emergence of Greek and Italian city-states, 700–500 BC

600 BC   Expulsion of tyrants from Athens and establishment of
democracy, 510–508 BC
Expulsion of kings from Rome and establishment of
republic, 509 BC

500 BC   Death of Hieron, tyrant of Syracuse, and "invention"
of rhetoric by Korax, 466 BC
Sophists active throughout Greek world, especially in
Athens, approx. 460–380 BC
Peloponnesian War between Athens and Sparta,
431–404 BC
Pericles' Funeral Oration, 430 BC
Career of Alcibiades, approx 430–403 BC
Gorgias first visits Athens, 427 BC
Lysias begins career as logographos, 403 BC

400 BC   Socrates' trial and *Apology*, 399 BC
Plato, *Gorgias*, approx. 380 BC
Plato, *Phaedrus*, approx. 375 BC
Isocrates, *To Nicocles*, approx. 372 BC
Isocrates, *Nicocles*, approx. 368 BC
Demosthenes, *For the Megalopolitans*, 352 BC
Isocrates, *Panathenaicus*, 342–339 BC

Demosthenes, *On the Chersonese*, 341 BC

Battle of Chaeronea leads to Macedonian domination of
   Greek city-states, 338 BC

Rhetoric for Alexander, 335 BC? (highly uncertain)

Demosthenes, *On the Crown*, 330 BC

Aristotle, *Rhetoric*, earlier than 322 BC

Death of Alexander the Great, beginning of Hellenistic
   period, 323 BC

Censorship of Appius Claudius the Blind (at Rome),
   312 BC

300 BC   Punic Wars between Rome and Carthage, 264–146 BC

200 BC   Consulship of Cato the Elder, 195 BC

Hermagoras, *On Invention*, approx. 150 BC

Establishment of Roman rule over Greek city-states of
   Balkan peninsula and Asia Minor, 148–146 BC

Death of C. Sempronius Gracchus, 121 BC

100 BC   Social Wars between Rome and former Italian allies,
   90–89 BC

Rhetoric for Herennius, approx. 86–82 BC

Cicero, *On Invention*, approx. 84 BC

Cicero, *Against Verres*, 70 BC

Cicero, *In Defense of Cluentius*, 66 BC

Consulship of Cicero, Catilinarian Orations, speech
   In Defense of Murena, 63 BC

Cicero, *In Defense of Caelius*, 56 BC

Cicero, *On the Orator*, 55 BC

Cicero, *Orator* and *Brutus*, 46 BC

Assassination of Julius Caesar, 44 BC

Proscription and death of Cicero, 43 BC

Caesar Octavian renamed Augustus, beginning of
   Roman principate, 27 BC

1 AD   Seneca the Elder, *Controversiae* and *Suasoriae*,
   39–40 AD

Neronian Period, including Lucan's *Bellum Civile* and
   Petronius' *Satyricon*, 54–68 AD

Gospel of John, 90–100 AD

Quintilian, *Institutio Oratoria*, approx. 92–96 AD

Plutarch, *Parallel Lives* (including Demosthenes, Cicero,
   Pericles, Alcibiades), 96–120 AD

100 AD	Pliny, *Panegyricus*, 100 AD
	Tacitus, *Dialogue on the Orators*, later than 96 AD, perhaps 101–102 AD
	Aelius Aristides, *To Rome*, 155 AD
	Hermogenes, *On Types, On Issues, Method of Forcefulness*, late second century AD
300 AD	Libanius becomes professor of rhetoric at Antioch, 354
	Sopater, *Division of Questions* (themes for declamations), second half of fourth century
	St. Augustine, *On Christian Doctrine*, 396–427 (Book 4 in 427)
1400	Poggio Bracciolini discovers manuscript of Quintilian, 1416
	Life of Desiderius Erasmus, 1469–1536
1500	Baldassare Castiglione publishes *Book of the Courtier*, 1528
	Life of Petrus Ramus, 1515–72
1600	Establishment of British Royal Society, 1661
1700	French Revolution, 1789
1800	Friedrich Nietzsche, *Lectures on Rhetoric*, prepared 1872–3
	Nietzsche, "On Truth and Lying in a Non-Moral Sense," 1873
1900	C. Perelman and L. Olbrechts-Tyteca, *The New Rhetoric*, first published in French as *La Nouvelle rhétorique: traité de l'argumentation*, 1958
	S. Toulmin, *The Uses of Argument*, first published 1958
	Various writings on "neo-sophism," 1990s to present

1

Rhetoric and the State

All human communities differentiate between specialized and every-day modes of communication. The distinction orders the chaos implicit in human language, with its twin possibilities of deceiving listeners and imagining a social context at odds with the present one. Special speech, often developed as part of ritual, organizes the linguistic diversity of the community and articulates its shared beliefs and aspirations. Ancient legend encodes an awareness of the interconnection between community and special speech in the story of Zeus' defeat of the last and most serious threat to his realm, the monster Typhoeus, who is represented as a whirlwind of cacophonous noise. In Hesiod's *Theogony*, an early Greek poem celebrating the foundations of the cosmic and social order, Typhoeus stands in sharp contrast to the Muses, who sing and dance harmoniously, befriend kings, and initiate poets into the mysteries of song.

Rhetoric and oratory enter the picture as human communities organize themselves into recognizable states. They continue the ordering function of special speech; only now the order and the speech have taken on very particular forms. The social order has become one in which communities develop a governing apparatus and a sense of purpose independent of the authority and aspirations of individuals, no matter how powerful. The community self-consciously represents itself as having a history, that is to say a life story that transcends the limits of any one human life. Among the ancient Greeks and Romans, the emergence of the state is also associated with a claim to authority over a clearly defined geographical territory, an expectation of citizens' willingness to fight in defense of the interests of the larger group, and a delineation of privileges and rights at least in part on the basis of an individual's perceived contribution to the military strength of the community. As states coalesce, then, power comes to be regarded less as a characteristic of specific interactions and more as a distinct possession to be shared, distributed, fought over, increased, diminished, and so on.

This disembedding of power from a magical or religious context is both propelled by and in turn propels a disembedding of certain kinds of language from the larger realm of special speech. Prose becomes disassociated from poetry and song, and the capacity to shape the community through language becomes dispersed and decentered. Masters of special speech still claim an authorizing connection with the world beyond the here and now; but they assert that authority through argument, example, skilful display of linguistic technique, and force of personality rather than attributing it to the inspiration of the Muse. Their role in the community is both an extension of and a rival to the role of singers, poets, oracles, and magicians. And it is also both an extension of and a rival to the role of organized fighters. Awareness of this point, too, is clear from early poetry, which represents special speech as a shared activity of fighters (in the case of the *Iliad*) and of those former and potential fighters left behind when the company of able-bodied men has departed for the battle front (as in the early books of the *Odyssey*). The close association between oratory and status as citizen-soldier persists throughout Greco-Roman antiquity. In the Roman republic, for example, the term *libertas*, which we might be tempted to construe as equivalent to the modern notion of freedom of speech, in fact describes the privilege of free, adult males (i.e., those construed as contributing to the defense of the community) to participate in discussions concerning governance. And in the later Roman empire, the most common means of crossing the boundary from unprivileged (i.e., non-Roman) to privileged is through distinguished military service.

In a sense, then, rhetoric is the special speech of the state. It is also, in effect, the occupation of off-duty soldiers. This connection between companies of free men and the governance of the state through ritualized argument also helps to explain the notorious exclusion of women from the realm of rhetoric. Ancient rhetoricians and orators were perfectly aware of women's linguistic capacity: indeed, they often represented the restriction of linguistic chaos as comparable to the regulation of women and considered both essential for the smooth operation of the state. Women's exclusion from rhetoric matches their exclusion from the battle line.

Thus far we have considered rhetoric as an extension of special or ritual speech and, as such, as an activity that orders the community in the face of primordial chaos. But the chaos that rhetoric guards against is not just the abstract possibility of dispersal, disorganization, or disagreement: it is also the chaos of violent dispute and internal conflict. Hesiod's Muses stand in contrast not just to the random noise of Typhoeus but also, at least implicitly, to wicked kings who give bad judgments in favor of insolent relatives and neighbors. In other words, they (and their poet-initiate) are the prototype of both the deliberative orator (who offers advice on issues of state) and of the forensic or judicial speaker (who takes sides in a matter of law). As deliberator, the orator relies on his implicit association with military power; as disputant, he puts aside his potential to resolve a conflict through force in favor of a conflict of words. In so doing, he also participates in the salvation of the community, which risks being torn apart by a cycle of violence and revenge. The Athenian orator Demosthenes emphasizes this point when he explains that rather than taking vengeance against Meidias, who insulted him by slapping him at a public festival, he is seeking redress in court. He asks the court, in effect, to turn his personal self-restraint into a legal precedent so as to encourage other victims of wrong to respond with litigation instead of further violence. In a more dramatic case, one involving not slaps and loss of prestige, but murder, enslavement, and exile, Cicero asks a Roman court to put an end to a village feud that has spun out of control by acquitting his client Cluentius of a charge of bribing a jury in a previous capital case. Cicero's case hinges on a distinction between the orderly processes of the Roman court and the violence and unpredictability of extra-legal procedures; in effect, he accuses his opponents of bringing the violence of blood-feud into the courtroom, and represents himself and his client as bulwarks of order against rampant social chaos. The arguments of Demosthenes and Cicero are obviously self-serving, but that does not render them invalid. The orators' commitment to processes of non-violent conflict resolution makes of them, for all their apparent elitism, champions of those who are in no position to prevail through force.

In its relationship to the state, rhetoric extends the authority of the warrior class while inviting the warrior class to behave less like warriors. In Athens as in Rome, mastery of special speech is a virtual prerequisite for full participation in the life of the community. A citizen regularly engages in rhetorical practice – as either speaker or listener, litigant or juror. Even the rise of specialized speech-writers at Athens, or the reliance on well-connected patrons at Rome, is indicative of the importance of rhetorical speech and of the need to master it, either directly or indirectly. Rhetoric creates a sense of inclusion among its participants. It engages them in a shared set of practices through which decisions are made about the community as a whole and its individual members. It creates a body of shared references that make communication efficient while also reinforcing solidarity among the communicators. And it develops a set of recurrent arguments and examples that encourage individual members of an audience to place high value on the well-being of the community in whose behalf the orator claims to speak.

As with any process of inclusion, there is, in the case of rhetoric, a corresponding set of exclusions. A group (in this case the body of citizens) is only a group if there are groups outside it. In a general sense, exclusion from the life of the city-state is reinforced through rules as to who may or may not speak in political and judicial processes. Throughout all of Athenian history women, slaves, and foreigners are denied the privilege of rhetorical speech; and for almost all of Athenian history the same applies to resident aliens – long-term immigrants, as it were, who often play a key role in the life of the community. In Rome, as we have already seen, free speech is in effect a kind of seigneurial privilege, the right of leading men in the community to offer advice on matters of general interest. Yet as often in Roman culture, the boundaries between an in-group and an out-group are negotiated through practice rather than enforced by law. Thus we hear of female orators, although their skill is either belittled by their male counterparts or attributed to their close relationship with distinguished fathers. Over time orators from beyond the confines of the city of Rome come to achieve influence, respect, and even renown. Yet their movement toward the center of power (both figuratively and literally) meets with resistance under the guise of redefinition of the form and content of special speech. Strictures on grammar, pronunciation, and gesture, far from being dry academic exercises, constitute ever-evolving standards for membership in the fraternity of those whose voices matter. Public speakers are continually called upon to prove their legitimacy as speakers even as they speak.

This question of the relationship between rhetorical style and legitimacy of voice is an important one, and we should pause for a moment to consider it in more detail. Anthropologists who have studied the role of formalized speech in a wide range of cultures come to two very different conclusions about its relationship to the processes of inclusion and exclusion. Some represent formalized speech as a strategy through which those in power create barriers against those out of power: a speaker can be ignored, ridiculed, disdained, or shouted down because of his perceived inadequacy as a speaker; the voices of women can be silenced by denying women a rhetorical education. We might consider the way even today mastery of a particular version of the English language is regarded as a *de facto* prerequisite for full membership in the economic and political life of the American and British communities. But others contend that formalization makes possible the very existence of the community, that it is, in effect, an evolutionary strategy through which human communities regulate their potentially limitless permutations. In their view (and here too we note a parallel with contemporary political and social debate), the standardization implicit in the construction of formalized patterns of speaking provides an opportunity for those outside the inner circle of power to enter it.

The dichotomy between the two positions is perhaps not as sharp as it seems – and indeed the study of ancient rhetoric lends support to both sides of the debate. In effect, the position of the second group, the evolutionists, is correct in the abstract or when the existence of the community as a whole is at stake. Indeed, some of the most memorable pages of Greek and Latin literature describe the chaos that ensues when principles of shared speech collapse, as in the class warfare, or stasis, that breaks out within and among Greek cities in the late fifth century BC, or in the internecine struggles of the Roman elite in the early years of the principate. For the Greek historian Thucydides, a striking feature of the breakdown of the city-state is the instability of language. For the Roman historian Tacitus, a defining characteristic of the corrupt state of affairs at Rome is the unreliability of formal speech, especially the gap between meaning and expression, and the increasingly restricted opportunities for its performance. To be sure, neither Thucydides nor Tacitus is concerned precisely with the problem of violation of formal guidelines for shaping speech. Yet their disturbing narratives do underscore the close relationship between the shared practice of formal discourse and the possibility of shared communal enterprise, even among those whose interests differ widely.

On the other hand, despite the indispensability of formal speech to the emergence and continued existence of recognizable communities, it is nonetheless clear that at any given historical moment those who have mastered the formalities are inclined to use them to maintain their mastery at the expense of others. We may view this tendency as a sad fact of human nature, or, more narrowly, as a characteristic of the particular shape of ancient societies and their later imitators. In effect, both Greece and Rome are societies constructed around honor and shame, with public speaking constituting a key means through which the former is accumulated and the latter (hopefully) avoided. And while some ancient thinkers allow for the possibility that the net honor of the community can be increased through the combined excellence of its individual members, by and large Greek and Roman men behave as if the competition for honor and shame were a zero-sum game: an increase in my honor means a decrease in yours. As a consequence, the citizen who has mastered the art of special speech has little incentive to use it in such a way as to augment the honor of fellow citizens. Far from it, he seeks the aggrandizement of himself or his faction at the expense of others, unless he is speaking to outsiders as well, in which case he may seek to augment his community's honor at the expense of theirs. Speechmaking becomes part of a culture of strategic performance in which observance of protocols of manliness and almost obsessive concern with the decorous presentation of the body mask an underlying and chronic anxiety over status, both in relationship to other males and, as free adult men, in relationship to all those whose voices have been silenced. For all of rhetoric's long-term function as a replacement or substitute for violent resolution of conflict, in the heat of the moment it tends to promote division, exclusion, and the maintenance of oppressive hierarchies, albeit through non-violent means.

Thus, for example, in one of the most famous speeches surviving from the corpus of Athenian oratory, Demosthenes defends a political ally for recommending that he be awarded an honorific crown by the city as a whole (hence the title, *On the Crown*). The very topic of dispute reveals the emphasis placed on outward expression of honor, even in the context of a supposedly egalitarian democracy. What is more, the body of the speech reveals Demosthenes – the great champion of democracy – ridiculing the chief prosecutor for the lowliness of his background in contrast to the (allegedly) lofty character and status of Demosthenes' own ancestors. Demosthenes' aim is to minimize the honor of his opponent in order to maximize that of himself and his associate. Indeed, as Cicero will tell us in one of his own invective speeches, the ideal outcome of an oratorical attack is to reduce the opposition to speechlessness: "I wanted to see you abject, contemned, disdained by everybody else, despaired of and abandoned by your very self. I wanted to see you suspicious . . . fearful, lacking confidence in your own resources, without voice, without freedom to speak, without influence, . . . shuddering, trembling, fawning on everyone. And that's what I saw" (*Against Piso* 99). Silencing an opponent, reducing him to social nullity, is the intended outcome of an unexpectedly high percentage of surviving speeches. As the Roman legal historian David Daube has noted, ancient city-states were in many ways like Victorian men's clubs (or for that matter, modern fraternities and sororities), and every debate was in effect a debate over membership. Since both Athens and Rome lacked public prosecutors, criminal trials were, by definition, a means of pursuing private ends. At the height of the Roman republic, for example, as many as one in three top officials were charged with crimes that could lead to loss of political rights, with the chance of conviction roughly fifty-fifty.

The oppressive use of rhetorical speech can be directed against whole sectors of society as well as against individual rivals. Throughout the tradition, this aspect is implicit in the repeated accusations of effeminacy, unmanliness, or servility: although directed against male rivals in an attempt to dishonor them, such charges of course reinforce the boundaries between men and women, freeborn and slaves. In Athens, such exclusions help to establish and maintain the solidarity of the male citizen body. They serve much the same function in Rome, although there the straightforward divide between participants and non-participants is complicated by the creation of explicit hierarchies within the body of participants. Highly suggestive is Cicero's train of thought when he finds himself speculating as to whether there were orators in distant periods of Roman history from which no texts survive. He infers the existence of competent orators on the basis of stories of the expulsion of the kings, the completion of successful embassies, and the suppression of the common people's demands for greater power. One early orator "settled the discord" of the plebs; another "assuaged their passions" against the aristocracy; yet another, dressed in priestly robes, rushed from the sacrifice he was performing to the assembly place where he "halted the insurrection" of the plebeians against the patricians (Cicero, *Brutus* 54–7). Cicero's hypothetical reconstruction of early Roman rhetorical history fits his project in the here and now, which entails solidifying aristocratic resistance to populist and demagogic demands for land reform, expansion of the franchise, and so on. Indeed, in the late Roman republic we observe a tragic clash of the two key social functions of special speech: the use of speech as a means of excluding others from power undermines the use of speech as an alternative to violent resolution of disputes. Cicero's vision of the toga-clad consul fending off the imposition of martial law falls short in reality not because it is naive but because it is not idealistic enough. He cannot bring himself to imagine extending participation in the ordering processes of special speech to a broad enough cross-section of the Roman populace. Paradoxically, as we shall see in chapter 4 below, his own death at the hands of Antony's soldiers comes to be reinterpreted by later Romans as a foundation sacrifice for just such a practice of social inclusion and status mobility through literary and rhetorical education.

If there is one figure whose exclusion preoccupies speakers and writers throughout Greco-Roman antiquity, it is the tyrant. We have already alluded to Cicero's contention that Brutus, who drove the last king from Rome, was an eloquent man. As Cicero suggests, Brutus could not have driven out Tarquin, established the republic, and forced the abdication of his first colleague in the consulship without exercising the persuasive power of oratory. The historical accuracy of Cicero's claim is hard to judge and, in any event, of less interest here than its ideological import: for it corresponds to a widespread sense that the end of tyranny is the beginning of rhetoric, and vice versa. It is my contention that the ancient belief in the mutual exclusivity of tyranny and rhetoric is itself a variation on the wider theme of rhetoric's role in the foundation of the state. The figure of the tyrant, who is in a certain sense responsible for the existence of the state, haunts both its institutions and its characteristic mode of special speech. Without grasping the structural problem posed by tyranny, we cannot fully understand either the form or the content of ancient rhetorical discourse. Even today, we experience the ramifications of this obsession with tyranny, as in the expressed opposition of both right and left in American politics to "government intervention," despite the demonstrable successes thereof in ventures that enjoy a wide range of support.

Let us explore this complex of ideas in more detail, both for its own sake and as a way of understanding the evolving context of ancient rhetorical performance. Corresponding to Cicero's story of the founding role of Brutus as orator is a Greek anecdote situating the very invention of rhetoric in the aftermath of the destruction (by none other than Zeus!) of the Syracusan tyrants Gelon and Hieron. As one relatively late source explains, a man named Korax, who had previously been associated with the tyrant Hieron,

> came to persuade the crowd and to be heard, just as he was listened to while in Hieron's service. He observed how the people had produced an unsteady and disorderly state of affairs, and he thought that it was speech by which the course of human events was brought to order. He then contemplated turning the people toward and away from the proper course of action through speech. Coming into the assembly, where all the people had gathered together, he began first to appease the troublesome and turbulent element among them with obsequious and flattering words . . . After this, he began to soothe and silence the people and to speak as though telling a story, and after these things to summarize and call to mind concisely what had gone before and to bring before their eyes at a glance what had previously been said. These things he called "introduction," "narration," "argument," "digression," and "epilogue." By means of them he contrived to persuade the people just as he used to persuade one man.[1]

In the anecdote, Korax is imagined as inventing political oratory and rhetorical categories of production and analysis simultaneously, and as doing so in the context of the formation of a new political order. Yet what the anecdote incompletely suppresses is the extent to which the new order is dependent on the old order of the tyrant: Korax can speak as he does to the people because he used to speak in such a manner to the tyrant; more important, the people conceive of themselves as a people and gather together in the assembly presumably because they had been conditioned to do so by the very tyrants who have just been removed from the scene.

While details of the anecdote are no doubt fictional, the association of the early state with a period of tyranny is grounded in historical reality. Many Greek city-states went through a period of tyrannical rule. The concentration of power in the hands of the tyrant and his supporters facilitated the concentration of power in the state more generally at the expense of the otherwise dominant aristocratic clans. Indeed, in the historian Herodotus' account of the evolution of the Athenian state, the rule of the Peisistratid tyrants is presented as enabling the rise of the demos. At Rome as well, scholars are increasingly inclined to regard the era of the kings, especially the late kings known as Tarquins, as one in which Rome's identity as a distinct community became fixed through the political and cultural efforts of a movement akin to Greek tyranny. Indeed, the persistent Roman hostility to the very term "king" (Latin, *rex*) corresponds to Greek discomfort with "tyrant," which is for writers throughout the centuries something of a fighting word.

As Greek democracy evolved, the figure of the tyrant remained an equally powerful bogeyman for aristocrats and commoners alike. To the descendants of the leading families, even as they participated in the life of the democracy, the tyrant served as a reminder that their power had once been wrested from them. Hence, over and over again, the tyrant (despite his name) appears in stories as a promoter of egalitarian justice. To the democrats, on the other hand, the figure of the tyrant serves as a reminder that the state or polis can exist without their governance: he lends the lie to the imagined naturalness of their rule. Indeed, throughout the history of Athenian democracy, one of the only figures to speak of the tyrant in neutral, even favorable terms, is the rhetorician Isocrates, especially when he represents himself as writing to kings. Isocrates is, in effect, the exception that proves the rule, for he seems to want to situate himself as an adviser to powerful figures who might unite the embattled Greek city-states. He imagines a position for himself not dissimilar to that assigned by our anecdote on the invention of rhetoric to Korax *before* the collapse of tyranny at Syracuse. Isocrates is thus the ancient prototype of one of the most consistent opponents of democratic speech throughout history: namely, the insider who imagines that his expertise can and should give him privileged access to the corridors of power.

In Rome, the political aspect of anti-tyrannical or anti-regal rhetoric plays out a little differently, but it still conforms to the pattern whereby the tyrant is transformed into a scapegoat whose expulsion secures the well-being of the community. Indeed, in one account of the early years of Rome, which seems to have circulated around the time of the assassination of Julius Caesar, Romulus, the legendary founder of the city, is himself cut into pieces by the members of the senate. Without Romulus there is no Rome, yet with him there can be no libertas, no free and open deliberation among the in-group of elite males. In the late republic, Cicero builds his career in part by railing against the real or alleged despotic behavior of other members of the Roman elite: first Sulla, whom he attacks indirectly through a case involving one of his henchmen; then the corrupt governor Verres, in effect a tyrant in his own province (perhaps not coincidentally, the province of Sicily, home to paradigmatic tyrants in Greek tradition); then, in succession, political rivals Catiline, Clodius, and finally Mark Antony. In the case of the last mentioned, Cicero reanimates the ghost of the Athenian orator Demosthenes, modeling his own resistance to an internal tyrant-in-the making on Demosthenes' attempt to rally the Athenians against the external threat posed by Philip of Macedon. The point, of course, is to brand Antony, like Catiline and Clodius before him, as in essence un-Roman. Their ascent to power would, in Cicero's presentation of the prospect, constitute not a change of personnel, but an end of the state as he and his contemporaries know it.

It is not surprising that this preoccupation with the figure of the tyrant continues into the era of the Roman principate. What is surprising is the extent to which scholars and others continue to take literary and rhetorical attacks on tyrants at face value. For the free, elite male, the concentration of power in the household of the emperor did mean a diminution of his own status – although not necessarily of his own wealth, or his own power with respect to other members of society. And it certainly did not mean the humiliation of the masses of provincials and freedmen throughout the territory of the empire: nothing comparable to the abject silencing of the Syracusans attributed to Gelon and Hieron, who allegedly forbade their citizens to speak altogether. To the contrary, the principate witnessed a relative increase in social mobility within the Roman world, as provincials, foreigners, and ex-slaves assumed increasingly important roles in the social, economic, and political life of Rome. In a sense, with the development of the principate we have a recreation of the state, once again following the pattern of the reduction of the power of aristocratic clans through the efforts of individual strongmen and their associates (in this case the emperors, their household staff, and loyal guards). And once again, the very beneficiaries of the new status quo are the ones most likely to be troubled by their dependence on the achievements, past or present, real or symbolic, of individuals they represent as "tyrants."

And so, in the very first generation of the principate, we find Seneca the Elder, in his memoirs of the schools of declamation, discussing case after case in which illicit, rapacious, and unmotivated actions by tyrants constitute the backstory for matters under debate. If we are to believe Seneca, Roman youths were trained on, and Roman adults displayed their rhetorical prowess through, discussion of the incomparably wicked behavior of tyrants. Such training obviously had an effect, inasmuch as later Roman authors, including Seneca's son, the philosopher and playwright known as Seneca the Younger, his grand-nephew, the epic poet Lucan, and the most distinguished historian of the imperial era, Tacitus, repeatedly organize their narratives around polarities of tyranny and resistance and introduce into them elements of the long-standing tradition of tyrant-bashing. Curiously, these very authors also give evidence of pursuing in their own careers a strategy more akin to that of Isocrates. That is, they present themselves as experts who merit the attention of the very rulers they characterize as real or potential tyrants. Tacitus serves as consul, the highest magistracy in the state, and in historical writing on earlier periods of the Roman principate subtly addresses contemporary issues and problems. And Seneca ends up as tutor and, in effect, regent of the emperor Nero on the basis of the renown he achieved in a variety of areas of cultural production.

Indeed, one of the key works of the imperial rhetorical tradition, Tacitus' *Dialogue on Orators*, assigns to an interlocutor the argument that the health of Roman society is inversely related to the presence of great oratory. As he puts it, "What need is there of long speeches in the senate when the best men swiftly arrive at agreement? What need of multiple harangues before the people when it's not the ignorant multitude that deliberates about the commonwealth, but a single man excelling in wisdom?" (Tacitus, *Dialogue* 41.4). There is an intentional irony in the assignment of this point of view to the character Maternus, who is earlier represented as lying low because of the political stir caused by presentation of his tragedy on the republican hero Cato. (And indeed, Tacitus may have based the fictional character Maternus on a historical figure of the same name who was executed by the emperor Domitian – see Dio 67.12.5). Yet none of the positions Tacitus assigns to his characters in the *Dialogue* seems historically implausible, although other interlocutors debate the somewhat less controversial question of whether oratory or poetry offers greater prospects of glory. Moreover, Maternus' summary statement implies not just acquiescence in the rule of one man, but contempt for the decision-making capabilities of the larger populace: what he deems, in an expression that echoes throughout Tacitus' historical writing, "an ignorant multitude." It is not that rhetoric has disappeared from Roman life: after all, speeches are still made in the senate, in the courts, on embassies, and so forth, and rhetorical language permeates all the literary genres of the period. But the masters of special speech have now accepted a restricted context for their performance in exchange for the security of the social pyramid and, we should note, of their place at or near its top.

Ideology is never just a reflection of current circumstances: it is also a productive force that generates and sustains transformation. The ideology of anti-tyranny that we have been considering motivates the institutions that form the context for political oratory at both Athens and Rome. In the case of Athens, resistance to tyranny takes the form of vigilant protection of the prerogatives of the demos, or mass of free citizens. Isonomia, what we might loosely translate as "equality by convention" (in contrast to obvious inequalities in talent, resources, etc.) and isegoria, equal right to speak in public, are extended by the Athenians to all citizen males. The peculiar institution of ostracism, by which an overly powerful citizen can be sent into exile for ten years, without even being charged with a crime, is but one of the mechanisms whereby the demos protects itself from the return of the tyrant. The Athenians develop a democratic system that acknowledges the claims of both common people and aristocrats and integrates them into a shared culture in part because both sectors have a stake in preventing the return of tyranny. In Rome as well, characteristic political institutions of the republic can be understood as devices for preventing the concentration of power in the hands of an individual: for example, the requirement that key magistracies be held by more than one person at a time; the strict limitation on the term of office of a dictator, even in times of crisis. Even with the return of monarchy in the person of Augustus, the chosen title, princeps, describes in a technical sense the most prestigious member of the aristocratic senate, in a more general sense, the "first-dibs-taker" in the carving of meat at a ritual sacrifice. There can be no princeps without a body of participes, and indeed no emperor seriously considers suspending or eliminating the senate.

What, then, are the contexts in which rhetorical speech is practiced at Greece and Rome? We have already mentioned trials and deliberations on policy; to these can be added embassies; funerals and other ceremonies that might call for speeches of praise or blame; and the election or recall of public officials, including, in both Athens and republican Rome, officials charged with the prosecution of wars. Jury trials in both societies could be quite large: we hear of Athenian juries as large as 6,000. Audiences in deliberative proceedings might be even larger. At Athens, every citizen had a right to participate in the meetings of the ekklesia, or assembly, which, not surprisingly, had to be held in an open air venue such as the Theater of Dionysus beneath the Acropolis, or on the nearby Pnyx. In Rome, meetings of the senate were restricted to members – still a goodly number, as many as a thousand in the time of the second triumvirate. Informal meetings, known as contiones, were called by magistrates to solicit input on matters under consideration by the senate or assemblies, to rally support for a cause, or to engage in grandstanding, and were governed by rules set by the convener. They did not have to be held in a consecrated space, as did meetings of the senate and electoral assemblies, and from what we hear could be very well attended and somewhat less than orderly. Meetings of Roman assemblies, and other gatherings, could be addressed from the Rostra, or speakers' platform in the forum. Criminal and civil trials, at least during the republic, also took place at various public sites throughout the forum. While we should probably not imagine gatherings of the size implied by Hollywood spectaculars, which tend to exaggerate the spaciousness of public spaces at Rome, nonetheless it was possible for a sizeable crowd to be in some sense present at virtually all political and judicial proceedings. Indeed, the orators themselves liked to imagine that the size of the crowd gathered at the senate door or the foot of the Rostra was a direct indication of a speaker's talent and following.

Theoretically, any citizen, in Athens as in Rome, could find himself in the position of addressing at least some political or legal gathering. In practice it seems that smaller numbers of the ambitious, the influential, or the opinionated, dominated the speakers' lists. Indeed, it has been suggested that the Greek word *rhêtor* first applied to those who were in the habit of making motions before the Athenian assembly. At Rome the term *patronus*, which in a broader social framework refers to the more influential or more highly honored partner in a relationship, comes to describe any speaker in a judicial proceeding. If opportunities for addressing the assembled people on official political business diminished under the Roman empire, the impulse for theatrical self-presentation did not. The more restricted environment of the literary recitation or the contest in declamation still drew crowds and served as a context for competitive display; in time, the custom of holding competitions in speechmaking (along with competition in musical performance and other skills) in outdoor theaters spread throughout the empire. Such display speeches continue the traditional association between mastery of special speech and the acquisition of honor. And perhaps more than is generally acknowledged they performed a political role as well. If the so-called sophists who delivered these speeches did not always address urgent concerns of policy, nonetheless their performances negotiated issues of ethnic identity, relations between cities, deference to imperial might, and so forth. And if their orations sometimes resulted in valuable prizes, so too did Demosthenes' many years of service to the Athenian demos earn him a golden crown (which he got to keep!).

Political and social conditions changed dramatically from the founding of the Greek city-states to the fall of the Roman empire. But throughout that millennium of history, mastery of rhetorical speech united communities small and large, substituted for violent resolution of conflict and dispute, served as an identifying mark of political leadership, differentiated the free community from tyranny, and in time provided a medium for renewal of the leadership class and for communication across boundaries of space, time, and ethnicity.

2

The Figure of the Orator

Narratives of ancient history tend to cluster around figures of great men (and some women): Socrates, Alexander, Pompey, Caesar, Cleopatra, and Nero are among the most famous. More recent trends in historical study discourage focus on strong individuals, and for good reason. History is as much about the processes attested by anonymous archeological remains, or implied in the shifting patterns of meaning to be traced through careful study of surviving texts, as it is about the triumphs and tribulations of strong individuals. But in the case of rhetoric and oratory, there is something to be said for a focus on the figure of the orator and on certain distinguished orators in particular. During his lifetime the orator stands alone: however much he may rely on friends and allies, slaves and research assistants, or paid claqueurs, when he speaks, all eyes and ears are on him. Indeed, given the size of many of the ancient audiences, the lack of artificial means of vocal amplification, and the potential distractions of a large crowd, a compelling presence was something of a prerequisite for participation in the practice of speechmaking. An Athenian or a Roman who wanted to influence decision-making in his respective society either brought to the process a preexistent charisma based on birth, wealth, or high achievement, or he generated it through his oratorical performance.

At the same time, the observable ability of some orators to sway the audience more than others, to hold the attention of the population time and time again, to pull off unexpected victories in trials or shape policy in consequential ways, transformed them into heroic exemplars for succeeding generations. The more complex and nuanced the process of speechifying became, the longer an apprenticeship it required. The longer the apprenticeship, the greater the need for something to aspire to. And so in both the Greek and the Latin tradition, certain orators came to figure, not just as models of style, but also as prototypes of ethical and political action and foundation myths for rhetorical education itself. In this chapter, then, we consider the figure of the orator in both general and specific terms: his education and accomplishments, successes, failures, and challenges, and his afterlife as a figure of praise – and sometimes blame – among succeeding generations. As we shall see, the orator, even as he lives, comes to occupy a position not entirely dissimilar to that of the tyrant within the imagination of the community. Not that the orator is accused of hideous crimes or treated as a type to be avoided at all costs; rather, individual orators, precisely because they speak for and to the larger society, come to embody the contradictions and tensions that pervade that society and to pay a heavy cost for doing so. Thus it should be no surprise that four of the five orators whose stories will form the basis of discussion in this chapter died violent deaths in contexts of civil or military strife.

The Athenian statesman Pericles is a good example of an orator whose status was both ascribed and achieved: ascribed in that he was descended from an aristocratic line, and therefore expected to take a leading role in the life of the community, achieved in that through skilful maneuvering and compelling self-presentation he became, in the view of some ancients, the veritable ruler of the Athenians, even as he abided by and celebrated the rules and culture of the radical democracy. Little of Pericles' oratory survives directly, but the version of his Funeral Oration preserved in the history of the Peloponnesian War composed by his younger contemporary Thucydides is one of the most famous and influential pieces of ancient writing. The occasion of the speech was the public funeral of the first year's casualties in what was to become an almost thirty year struggle between the Athenian empire and Sparta and its allies. In accordance with Athenian custom, an influential individual chosen by the state delivered the eulogy of the dead. By the outbreak of the war, Pericles had already shaped Athenian policy both externally and internally. It was he who encouraged Athens to use the resources of her empire to construct the monumental public works that organized and beautified the city; and it was he (according to Thucydides) who had persuaded the Athenians to abandon their rural territory to the invading Spartans and to rely instead on the strength of their city walls and the invincibility of their fleet.

As scholars have noted, for all that Pericles' Funeral Oration provides a lofty vision of the accomplishments and spirit of democratic
Athens, it does so by ascribing to the population at large the qualities
traditionally associated with aristocrats. Pericles praises Athens through
its ancestors, both distant and near, especially those who expanded its
patrimony. He characterizes the Athenians as ennobled by a sense of
ease mingled with obligation toward the less fortunate. The Athenians'
military prowess, he asserts, is due to their singular nature, rather
than to relentless, laborious discipline of the sort imposed on Spartans.
Even the poor suffer no disgrace at Athens, provided they struggle
against their poverty; even the workers "are fair judges of public
matters," and those who cannot originate action are nonetheless
capable of evaluating it. As for the dead, according to Pericles they
met their fate not in a lowly or necessary struggle of self-defense, but
with the goal of wreaking vengeance on their enemies and acquiring
honor for themselves. Virtually every point in Pericles' speech can be
paralleled in the self-aggrandizing rhetoric of earlier aristocrats. That
the speech has often been read as embodying a model of democratic
idealism is a tribute to its own seductive power; but also, perhaps, a
testimony to the corruption or insecurity of democratic values throughout the ages. It is hard to imagine anyone who genuinely valued all
human beings equally, regardless of "honor," "excellence," or "ease
of manner," wanting to recreate Athens just as Pericles depicts it in
his famous oration.

In a sense, then, Pericles works from within the Athenian democracy
to redefine it. He uses a democratic occasion and democratic procedure to foster an Athenian sense of self that is more *noblesse oblige*
than "one man one vote." Many readers of Thucydides have interpreted the speech as tragically ironic, not because of its conflation of
democratic and aristocratic values, but because its presentation is soon
followed by the narrative of the disastrous plague that devastated the
Athenian population. In their view, the tragedy and the irony are only
intensified in that the suffering of the Athenians is compounded,
perhaps even caused, by their adherence to Pericles' advice to gather
within the city walls.

But there is another way of interpreting the relationship between
the Funeral Oration and the succeeding narrative of the Peloponnesian
War. In effect, the oration helps us to understand how the Athenians
survived the disasters inflicted upon them during the course of many
years of war. It shapes the Athenians as idealized aristocrats in spirit

and in practice, capable of holding out against the Spartans even as their territory is ravaged, their allies abandon them, and their own leaders propel them to catastrophic choices. Indeed, some of the clearest echoes of the Funeral Oration are to be found in Thucydides' descriptions of the Athenians' reactions to catastrophe: the vigor with which they defended the city even while manning the grandiose expedition against Sicily (7.28); the doomed general Nicias' insistence that even in the face of overwhelming odds the Athenians have it in them to recover and to restore their city's power (7.78); Thucydides' own observation that despite their panic and despair at the loss of the Sicilian Expedition, the members of the Athenian demos, "as is their habit, were ready to manage everything in an orderly manner" (8.1); and his summary reflection to the effect that of all Athens' enemies it was the Syracusans, who most resembled them in spirit, who did them the most harm (8.97). To be sure, Thucydides recognizes the damage done to Athens by its demagogic orators and the risks inherent in its system of governance; but alongside the risks he sees positive outcomes as well, including Pericles' shaping of the Athenian spirit – an achievement he cannot help admiring and invites his readers to admire as well. For him, Pericles creates through oratory a vision that inspires Athenians to actions well beyond what can reasonably be expected of them.

Two generations after Pericles, the orator Demosthenes continues the Periclean practice of using oratory as a mean of advancing a cohesive political agenda, one that sustains and is sustained by a vivid vision of Athenian particularity. More than Pericles, Demosthenes relies on speeches in court as well as in the assembly and council. And if we are to believe the ancient biographical tradition, much more than was the case with Pericles, Demosthenes' political and oratorical preeminence was achieved by effort, rather than ascribed by birth. We are told that Demosthenes was cheated of a significant portion of his inheritance by dishonest relatives; that he was sickly and retiring as a youth; that his voice was weak. We are also told that he overcame such obstacles through persistence, hard work, and some rather drastic forms of self-discipline. For example, one anecdote recounts that he shaved half his head so that he would be too embarrassed to leave his underground study until he had learned proper techniques of dramatic delivery – at which point, apparently, his hair would be long enough that he could cut both halves to the same fashionable length (Plutarch, *Life of Demosthenes* 7.3). Of course, such a story nicely corresponds to the political vision advanced by Demosthenes – one in which Athens, through discipline, patience, and occasional drastic action will maintain its autonomy in an Eastern Mediterranean world increasingly dominated by the aggressive impulses of Macedon, a neighboring kingdom led first by Philip, then, late in Demosthenes' life, by his son Alexander the Great.

Indeed, to read Demosthenes' speeches against the backdrop of Pericles' Funeral Oration is to see how skillfully Demosthenes redefines Athenian identity to fit changing circumstances even as he evokes visions of Athens' Periclean imperial past. For example, in a relatively early speech, *For the Megalopolitans*, Demosthenes intervenes in a debate as to which of two antagonistic cities Athens should support – Megalopolis or Sparta? The choice is complicated by the fact that while Sparta is a long-standing rival of Athens, it has recently allied with it in a conflict against Thebes, whereas Megalopolis, which has done nothing to offend Athens on its own, is nonetheless in alliance with Thebes, which is at present openly hostile to Athens. The overall recommendation of Demosthenes is that Athens should promise to support Megalopolis if Sparta takes action against it, not for love of Megalopolis, but as an expression of a general principle of opposition to aggression and out of particular concern that should Sparta conquer Megalopolis it would threaten a genuine Athenian ally, Messene.

What interests us here is the way Demosthenes introduces his argument. At the outset of the speech he suggests that those who have addressed the assembly before him in support of either Megalopolis or Sparta have abused each other verbally, "just as if they really were ambassadors from either side, rather than your fellow citizens" (*For the Megalopolitans* 1). They have, in his view, assimilated themselves to the visiting delegations with whom they side: as he puts it, "if it weren't for familiarity with the speakers and their use of the Attic language, most people would assume that one party is Arcadian and the other Spartan" (*For the Megalopolitans* 2). In contrast, Demosthenes presents himself as concerned only with Athenian interests, both short and long term.

Demosthenes' opening gambit may seem an obvious one – he distances himself from all who have preceded and presents himself as the voice of Athens and therefore singularly worthy of the Athenians' attention. But the strategy is a little more complex than that. On the one hand, by calling attention to earlier speakers' absorption in the interests of Sparta and Megalopolis, Demosthenes makes it clear that the interests of city-states can be (and in this case most decidedly are) radically different and all-consuming. If this is the case for other city-states, then surely it is the case for Athens as well: hence the task of the Athenians is to be as self-absorbed and self-interested as citizens of other city-states, even if the issue may not seem as pressing as the potential war facing Sparta and Megalopolis. Unlike Pericles, Demosthenes appeals not to the intrinsic differences between Athens and other city-states, but to implicit similarities: all are on the lookout for their own interests. Yet, at the same time, this very situation necessitates of the Athenian assembly an unwavering attention to the history, standing, principles, needs, and desires of Athens. And so Demosthenes, like Pericles before him, will end up examining the particularities of Athenian experience and using them to develop and advance an argument for a given course of action.

Demosthenes' ability to articulate Athens' needs and interests paradoxically emerges, in the same passage, from the experience of Athenian rhetoric. For in describing the prior Athenian speakers as being indistinguishable from the Megalopolitans and Spartans whose interests they represent, Demosthenes alludes to an obvious outcome of rhetorical training (and one that has perennially troubled its opponents), namely, the ability to speak with conviction on either side of an issue. In effect, Demosthenes proposes a meta-rhetoric, an ability to see beyond and through the rhetorical strategies of his rivals. But this meta-rhetorical pose is itself a product of rhetorical thinking and a compelling rhetorical strategy. Indeed, we might say that it is the predominant strategy of Demosthenes' political career, since over and over again throughout the speeches on public issues Demosthenes presents himself less as advocate for a cause than as analyst of others' arguments. At the level of the sentence, this concern with balanced analysis manifests itself in a strong predilection for antithetical constructions – so strong that, according to one source, it was mocked onstage as part of a comic performance. More broadly, this concern with balance and discernment characterizes Demosthenes' relentlessly logical consideration of any and all possible courses of action facing his audience in their immediate circumstances.

None of this is to suggest that Demosthenes always advised the Athenians wisely, or that he was any more or less sincere than those who held alternative points of view. Rather, what is striking about the surviving texts of Demosthenic oratory is how the ethos, or character, he projects situates him both inside and outside the immediate context:

inside, in that he evinces genuine concern for the well-being of the Athenians as Athenians; outside, in that he sees enough of the rest of the world and its workings to know what differentiates Athenian interests from those of other city-states. In this sense Demosthenes pushes beyond Periclean rhetoric to construct a vision of Athens that is not so much essentialist as relativistic. This Demosthenic ethos is decidedly well suited to a democracy, since it invites individual Athenians to view themselves from the outside, not as spectators, but as potential possessors of other identities.

Demosthenes' capacity for analysis is found in various contexts. Thus, in his speech *On the Chersonese*, he expresses astonishment that other speakers can insist on a "simplistic distinction between war and peace" (*On the Chersonese* 4). Demosthenes' point seems to be that war and peace are not existential states that a city can enter or exit at will, but aspects of relationships between political entities that can be of diverse sorts and in any event are never determined by the actions of a single party. It is Demosthenes' ability to disassociate words from their emotional or value-laden context that, paradoxically, allows him to define the object of analysis more precisely. As he puts it in the same speech, if Philip continually violates the terms of the peace compact he made with the Athenians, then what does it even mean to say that we must choose "either war or peace"? (*On the Chersonese* 6). Is Athens at peace if Philip wages war against it? Is it warlike to resist aggression? Again, these are not sophistic or semantic games being played by Demosthenes, but an attempt to chart a course of action on the basis of analysis rather than sloganeering. Indeed, Demosthenes acknowledges that such an approach risks unpopularity since, in effect, it requires the Athenians to catch up with the orator who sees the difference between their desires and their interests.

But perhaps there is something disingenuous about the talk of risking unpopularity. For while Demosthenes' career experienced its setbacks (not all of them at the hands of the Athenian demos), he persisted in speaking publicly on a wide variety of issues. He was even more celebrated after his death than during his life, and one anecdote from among the many that accrued around him helps us to understand what both contemporary and later admirers found noteworthy about him. When challenged by other orators for not speaking extemporaneously but instead producing speeches that "smelled of the lamp" (i.e., involved much work late into the night), Demosthenes acknowledged the charge and observed that preparation showed respect for the people, while carelessness in speaking was a mark of an oligarchical personality, one who ultimately relied on force rather than persuasion. Whether the story is true or not, it corresponds to the sense a modern reader has in reading Demosthenic oratory in contrast to say contemporary political soundbites and press conferences, namely that Demosthenes actually expected the people, as jurors or deliberators, to follow, understand, and value careful, thorough explication of detailed matters – to be, as Nietzsche put it, good listeners as well as good speakers in their own right.

This respect for the demos may explain as well the suggestion, recurrent in the lore of Demosthenes, that while his speeches, when read, come across as simple, clear, and understated, his delivery of them was virtually ecstatic. Words like "forceful," "awe inspiring," even "possessed," are used by ancient writers to describe his impact on his audience. Demosthenes' admirers see in him the true heir of the inspired priests and poets of early Greece. But he achieves this position by further disembedding special speech from its ritualized origins. In effect, he becomes, like Cicero after him, a high priest of secular reason.

Consideration of one more Athenian orator puts in perspective the achievement of Pericles and Demosthenes, in particular their fostering of an analytic stance and approach that allows the orator to reshape the community from within. The orator in question is Alcibiades, arguably the sexiest figure in Greek politics, a man who seemed to be whatever his audience needed on any given occasion. Recovering the historical Alcibiades is less our concern here than understanding what Alcibiades meant to those Greeks, contemporary and later, who discussed him.

And discuss him they did – in comedies, speeches, histories, biographies, and eventually even in school exercises that invited students to sharpen their skills in praise and blame. His appearance in Plato's *Symposium*, where he crashes a party, but is welcomed nonetheless, and ends up transforming and, in spite of himself, deepening the import of the conversation that has been underway before his arrival, for all its brilliance and distinctiveness, conforms to the pattern of Alcibiades literature. Alcibiades is always just what is wanted. Even when he is accused of sacrilegious behavior in the days preceding the ill-fated Sicilian Expedition, the Athenians nonetheless insist that he continue as one of the commanders of the fleet, with his legal fate to be decided upon his return. When he connives with the Spartan ambassadors, they trust him, because he tells them what they need to hear. So too, when he addresses the Argives, and again in his relations with the Persian king. Indeed, Plutarch's story of Alcibiades' first appearance before the assembly anticipates the pattern of his relationship to his audience. As Plutarch has it, Alcibiades just happened to be in the vicinity when he heard the assembly making a hubbub; when he discovered that the uproar was in gratitude for another wealthy citizen's financial contribution to the polis, Alcibiades entered the assembly and made a sizeable contribution, too. So enthralled was he by the subsequent applause that he accidentally let slip a quail he just happened to be carrying under his robe. The bird flew off, the crowd grew even more excited and started to pursue, and the man who caught it became Alcibiades' lifelong friend (Plutarch, *Life of Alcibiades* 10.1).

The anecdote neatly encapsulates the appeal and the danger of Alcibidean rhetoric. Who could resist the spontaneous gesture and the competition in generosity to the city? Apparently not the demos, for they respond to Alcibiades' affection with affection of their own, matching his distractibility (where was he going with that quail? one wonders) with their own (what were they supposed to be doing next at the meeting when they turned instead to recovery of the bird?). In a sense, Alcibiades is the instantiation of the city talking to – and loving – itself. Not that there is anything unexpected about such a process. Indeed, that is what isegoria, or equal political participation, equal right to speak before the assembly, is all about: each man speaking in the city's interest to others listening in the city's interest. Plato's Socrates will describe such a process as flattery, assigning it an ethical or characterological dimension. But that seems to miss the more difficult problem that the tradition of Alcibiades lore is getting at: how does one get outside any system of discourse? How does one develop and maintain a sufficiently distinctive perspective to be able to contribute to the transformation of the city (or nation or society) without becoming too different to be heard? Socrates didn't solve the problem, not in his lifetime as his execution despite the performance of his *Apology* indicates, nor in his afterlife, since even Plato repeatedly speaks of his *atopia*, or "out-of-placeness." As I have tried to suggest, it is the orator who lives this struggle between immersion in the state and critique of it. And while the example of Alcibiades may warn him off too deep an investment in the erotics of talk, imitating Socrates leaves him nowhere.

In the Roman world the case of Cicero recapitulates the challenges and opportunities observable in Greek rhetoric, but with perhaps a greater degree of self-awareness, precisely because Cicero had before him the examples of Pericles, Demosthenes, Alcibiades, and others. Cicero is both a Roman priest of secular argument, one who seeks to establish a deep identification with traditions of prayer, incantation, and authorization from afar, and a self-aware student and consumer of a long-established system of rhetorical instruction and method. There is a knowingness about Cicero that makes many modern readers uncomfortable, leading even to charges of hypocrisy. But there is also an energy and passion, a human complexity, that has sustained interest throughout the ages and given rhetoric, if not quite a hero, then certainly an emblem of its potential role in civil society.

Born to a well-to-do but politically insignificant family in the small town of Arpinum, Cicero made his way to Rome as a young man during a period of heightened political and social tension. He entered upon a career of advocacy in an era when it was illegal for an orator to accept financial compensation for his efforts. On the one hand, this restriction can be understood as a way of preventing the powerful in society, especially members of the senatorial aristocracy, from taking advantage of those who desperately needed their help in negotiating the Roman legal system. On the other, it also served to forestall the development of rhetoric as a profession, a means of making a living the way one could make a living in ancient Rome from banking, farming, architecture, and so on. In effect, the ban on payment for oratory reinforced patterns of dependency: an individual or group of individuals under attack – through the legal process or otherwise – by the more powerful could only respond by seeking the assistance of someone else among the disproportionately powerful. What the weaker party could offer the stronger was, if not money, then loyalty, what the Romans called *gratia*, an implicit promise of support for the stronger party in situations in which he might require it – either instances in which he himself was under legal attack, or in support of his electoral ambitions.

Cicero, whose family wealth gave him the leisure (although he would not have called it that) to defend the interests of various weaker parties, took full advantage of the expectations of gratia, as he relied upon precisely those parties and their friends and allies to assist him in his own swift ascent of the Roman political ladder. Thus, we see him, throughout his career, defending the interests of those who are, relatively speaking, on the margins of Roman power. Perhaps the most spectacular example of this practice is his early prosecution of Verres for malfeasance during his governorship of Sicily, a prosecution that Cicero undertakes in defense of the numerous aggrieved Sicilians who, while they may have legal standing to bring charges against Verres, lack the prestige, connections, and perhaps rhetorical skill to represent their interests effectively before a Roman jury. They, like many Roman provincials before and after, entrust their case to a patron at Rome. By prosecuting it vigorously – so vigorously, we are told, that the defendant Verres left town after the first day of what was to have been a five-day presentation of the prosecution case by Cicero – Cicero earns not only the loyalty of those Sicilians who had been harassed by Verres, but also the potential support of all provincials and newcomers who find themselves placed at a disadvantage by the hierarchical, Rome-centered system of governance and administration.

This tactic of defending the relatively disadvantaged in moments of legal or political difficulty without seriously questioning the political and social structures that put them at a disadvantage allows Cicero to build a reliable base of political clients without entirely alienating the old aristocratic elite, the self-styled "best men" or optimates. Cicero is content to be the safety valve in a system that is dangerously close to explosion. As a result, he moves quickly through the political ranks, achieving each magistracy in the Roman administrative cursus at the earliest legal age – a process that culminates in his election as consul for the year 63 BC.

Precisely because Cicero is a new man, that is, the first holder of high office in his family, and because his fame is based purely on oratorical and legal, as opposed to military, achievements, his authority as consul is relatively weak. Any action he may wish to take requires the support of his uncooperative fellow consul (it was a distinctive feature of the Roman republic to have multiple simultaneous holders of the same office). And while Cicero has widespread electoral support, it is unclear how or even whether it is to be translated into a mandate for any particular sort of action. It is perhaps precisely because of this evident weakness in Cicero's position that two threats to the very system of government he represents make themselves felt during his consulate. One, close at hand, and quite possibly exaggerated by Cicero, is the so-called Catilinarian Conspiracy, a cabal of the disaffected led by a bankrupt aristocrat; the other, more distant, is the returning army led by the victorious general Pompey who, although a tentative political ally of Cicero, may well wish to take advantage of any unruliness in Rome to impose martial law, or worse, as his predecessors Marius and Sulla had done, much to the disadvantage of Roman republicanism, as well as to the thousands of individuals who lost life, property, or status as a result of their depredations. Faced with this double danger, Cicero plays one threat against the other, and in a series of astonishingly effective speeches, rallies the Roman senate and people to unite against the alleged conspirators, all the while reminding them that Pompey is making his way back home.

In Cicero's view, his success in rousting and, in a handful of cases, executing the Catilinarian conspirators, rescued the Roman state. And he may well be right, at least in the sense that his efforts granted the republican form of government a temporary reprieve. His handling of the conspiracy also affected the rest of his career, as it led to his exile for the illegal execution of the citizen-conspirators without trial, consolidated a dangerous them-against-us dimension of his political worldview, and resonated in every aspect of his later oratorical career, where he was forced to explain, for example, his defense of a man purported to have been assigned by Catiline to assassinate Cicero, or of another who had close social and political connections with Catiline and his supporters. Apart from their effect on Cicero's career and reputation, the speeches against Catiline illuminate three crucial aspects of the figure of the orator.

First, they demonstrate the ideal orator's easy versatility in adapting his style and argument to various audiences. The action against the Catilinarian conspirators entailed two speeches before the senate and two before the assembled Roman people over the course of a little more than a month, and it is readily apparent from the surviving texts that Cicero varied the emphasis in his argument depending on the audience as well as on the fast-changing political circumstances. He plays upon the aristocrat's fear of a breakdown of solidarity within the senatorial ranks and on the urban merchant's disdain (and perhaps envy) for the sophisticated lifestyle of the elite – one entailing all-night partying, extravagant expenditure, and violation of sexual norms. He reminds the senate of other instances in which members of their order behaved in a treacherous manner; before the people he summons images of tumultuous invasions of Italy and Rome, and reminds them that the threat they now face has been parried without a full-fledged call to arms.

Which leads to the second key aspect of Cicero's performance: his insistence that a unified people and aristocracy, under the vigorous leadership of a duly elected consul, operating in accordance with established legal procedures, can protect itself from menaces within and without. Years later, cynical Romans were to laugh at a line from Cicero's poem on his own consulate in which he declared "let weapons yield to the toga." They seem to have added, as a further joke, the even more awkward expression "let the laurel leaf give way to the tongue." But if Cicero's self-promotion in verse was slightly ludicrous, the contrast between a general in armor and a consul in the garb of peace was no laughing matter for a society that had witnessed (and would continue to witness) successive waves of proscription, mass execution, and political transformation at the hands of individual strongmen leading what were in effect private or personal armies. Cicero regarded his suppression of the Catilinarian Conspiracy and restoration of order, all while dressed in the garb of civilian magistracy, as a potential refoundation of Rome on principles of shared political participation. For all its overdramatization, the exemplary nature of Cicero's performance held the interest of successive generations of Romans, who turned to it time and again when faced with a choice between violent and verbal resolution of internal conflict.

Third, the speeches against Catiline exemplify Cicero's willingness to tap into the deepest passions and fears of what we might call the Roman collective unconscious. Greek orators, too, needed to be in touch with unarticulated concerns of the population and to conduct themselves in public in such a manner as to inspire confidence, hope, even love. But more than any other aspect of the ancient rhetorical tradition, Ciceronian oratory gives evidence of repeated eruptions of the primordial. When the historian Walter Burkert wrote that the Romans were in many ways closer in spirit to the neolithic age than to our own, I like to think that he had Ciceronian oratory in mind. While there can be no doubt that Cicero, in his oratory as in his philosophy, expresses the rationalizing spirit of the age, the eagerness to integrate the practical wisdom of Roman farmers and businessmen with the expertise of Greek specialists, to reconceptualize Roman tradition in terms of Greek models of knowledge, nevertheless his oratory time and time again conjures with forces that are beyond human control and calls upon the magical capability of the master of special speech.

In the Catilinarians, this interest in the primordial manifests itself in Cicero's orchestration of sacrificial imagery. Taking advantage of the consul's role in the performance of animal sacrifice at the commencement of a meeting of the senate, Cicero represents Catiline, first, as one excluded from the sacred circle of participants in the unifying rite of power over life and death, and subsequently, as the intended sacrificial victim of none other than Jupiter himself. Not content to depict his conflict with Catiline as a reprise of Romulus' execution of Remus, Cicero transforms Catiline into an outcast of the gods and his departure from Rome into an event of cosmic significance. Cicero seems to draw upon the experience – familiar to the Romans as a conquering people – of "calling out" a city's gods prior to obliteration of the human and physical remains. Through his speeches against Catiline he drives out the enemy of the gods in order to keep them secure in their Roman homes.

Cicero thus invokes the role of the orator as communicator with the world beyond – a role especially appropriate during his year as consul, since the consul is in effect both a political and a religious figure. Indeed, in a speech delivered at a trial held between the first and second speeches against Catiline, Cicero blurs the boundary between his personal status as speaker for the defense and his politico-religious status as consul right from the outset. The case involved a charge of bribery against Cicero's political ally, Murena, who had been elected to succeed him to the consulate. Were Murena to be convicted, he would not be allowed to hold office, a political outcome Cicero considered unacceptable. While the speech is often cited for Cicero's humorous dismissal of Murena's accusers, one for being an incomprehensible specialist in legal technicalities, the other, Cato the Younger, for being an overly scrupulous moralist, it is in fact the august opening that sets the overall tone of the proceedings. Cicero's language as he commences his defense of Murena perfectly recreates the ordering into stanzas, the careful shaping of individual phrases, and the interweaving of repeated words and sounds that also characterize surviving Roman prayers. And the content of this incantatory opening is a reminder to the audience, that he Cicero, as consul, delivered the prayer on behalf of Murena, at the time of his election to the consulate, which is now being challenged. Cicero's rhetoric works at a pre- or non-rational level to situate the audience in a relationship of congregants to presiding clergy, rather than jury to defense attorney. Indeed, the non-rational nature of his appeal is confirmed by the ending of the speech, where Cicero's language echoes perhaps the most famous speech in Roman history prior to his own career, namely Gaius Gracchus' mournful lament on the last day of his life. Cicero projects Murena into the position of Gracchus, imagining that he, like Gracchus, has nowhere to turn in his hour of need except to the Roman people. Never mind that the appeal did Gracchus no good – he was set upon by agents of the senate shortly after delivering the speech and killed in cold blood – nor that Gracchus, as a tribune promoting land reform, occupied a rather different position on the political spectrum than Cicero and Murena. What Cicero seems to be invoking is both sympathy for Murena and a sense of overwhelming crisis with only violence as an outcome – unless the jurors intervene in Murena's defense.

This appeal to the historical, and in some instances prehistorical, feelings and experiences of the Roman people characterizes speeches from outside the consular year as well. For example, in his defense in 56 BC of a younger protégé, Marcus Caelius Rufus, on a complex set of charges that could have led to Caelius' loss of citizen status, Cicero's strategy is to attack the motives of the prosecution. In particular, he suggests that the sister of his own political enemy, Publius Clodius Pulcher, is responsible for the most alarming charges, and that this sister, named Clodia, is only interested in taking vengeance on Caelius for their failed love affair. He attacks Clodia using a number of techniques, the most surprising being an impersonation of her long-dead ancestor Appius Claudius the Blind, who accuses her of failing to live up to the high moral standards set by her male and female ancestors alike. A later source tells us that in delivering the speech Cicero took on the bearing and voice of the blind censor, just as he took on the bearing and voice of Publius Clodius, whom he next impersonates, in order to criticize Clodia from another vantage point.[1] The impersonations point to the at-times close relationship between theater and oratory in the ancient world. Indeed, they form part of a complex pattern of allusion to comedy and tragedy alike throughout the speech, which culminates in Cicero's invitation to the jury/audience to give Caelius' travails a comic outcome, one restoring him to the embrace of the community. The contrast between the aged censor and the young Clodius anticipates Cicero's presentation of his relationship to Caelius as that of comic father to wayward comic son. But the verb used to describe the summoning of Appius Claudius is *excitare*, the technical term for the summoning of ghosts, whether in magical rites or in the representation thereof onstage. And Appius' own speech, with its proud list of accomplishments on the part of the Claudian clan, calls to mind another type of ritual performance, namely the wearing of death masks and impersonation of ancestors at aristocratic funerals. Indeed, the impersonation of Appius may not be aimed at Clodia at all, as much as at the jury, which would have consisted chiefly of representatives of families that did not have the ius imaginum, or right to keep and display death masks; in other words, men who may have felt a certain weariness or resentment at the constant reminders of the social superiority of the Clodii and their Claudian ancestors.

But another instance of calling forth the dead, again involving the Claudian gens or clan, has a more troubling feeling about it. Just a few years after his successful defense of Caelius against Clodia and, by implication, Clodius, Cicero found himself called upon to defend a political connection, T. Annius Milo, who was charged with the murder of Clodius. Milo and Clodius were leaders of rival gangs of political operatives and thugs, and a clash on the Appian Way had led to the death of the latter. Cicero devotes much of the surviving speech to a reasonably coherent defense of Milo on the grounds that Clodius had attacked him first. But partway through he changes tactics and begins to conjure with other possibilities. He attacks the character of Clodius; he suggests that even if Milo had appeared in Rome with bloodstained sword and proclaimed himself the murderer of Clodius he would have been greeted with praise and admiration for destroying the noxious pest; and he poses to the members of the jury a challenge: "Imagine if you will that I can persuade you to acquit Milo – but only on condition that Publius Clodius lives again. Why, look how frightened you've all become! Just the thought of the dead man terrifies you: how would you feel if he really did come back to life?" (*In Defense of Milo* 79). Later still in the speech, after declaring that it was the very hills and groves of Alba, even Jupiter of the Alban Mount, who had brought destruction on Clodius, he again raises the prospect of Clodius' reanimation, crying out to Clodius' supporters in the audience: "Go ahead, raise him up, raise him up from the dead if you are able!" But, he continues, in reference to the burning of the senate house that accompanied Clodius' funeral: "How will you break his assault once he is alive again, if you cannot control the avenging furies of his corpse?" (*In Defense of Milo* 91).

Is Cicero's evocation of Clodius just a vivid strategy for getting the jury to acknowledge that they are better off now that he is gone? Or does it rather play with the possibility that the dead can return, either directly as ghostly revenants, or indirectly, through the reanimation of prototypes on the part of descendants and followers? How is the corpse of Clodius to be laid to rest? And what would it mean for the state to punish Milo for killing, with malice aforethought or not, a man who threatened the well-being of the state? The surviving speech of Cicero is not the one he delivered: so tumultuous was the audience at the trial, that despite the presence of Pompey's soldiers to keep order, Cicero reined in his rhetoric – and Milo was convicted. For some reason, Cicero thought it important to get the revised version circulating among Roman readers (including, we are told, Milo himself, in exile in Massilium). No doubt Cicero wanted to burnish a reputation damaged by the conviction of Milo. But the content of the speech seems to reflect on the experience of the trial. In a sense, Clodius has returned to life, through the threatening behavior of the audience at the trial and in the election of Pompey as sole consul (a virtually unprecedented event in Roman history). Cicero's challenge – do you want Clodius to return? – speaks to readers and listeners beyond the context of the trial. It reminds us that the Roman state, like any state, must take control of its own history. In Rome, as in Athens, one way of doing so is by laying the dead to rest, rather than letting them wander restless and disruptive among the living. In Athens, the tradition of the funeral oration allowed Pericles to create a canonical interpretation of the lives of the recently deceased and in so doing to fashion a myth of Athens that sustained their survivors through the challenges to come. In the speech he delivered in defense of Milo, Cicero evidently failed to impose such an interpretation on the dead Clodius. And in the speech he published he makes clear that he understands the consequences of such failure for the well-being of Rome.

If images of blood sacrifice and avenging gods and instances of evocation of the dead show Cicero grappling to control and channel forces we are inclined to describe as supernatural, at least one speech illustrates the reverse process, that is the ascription to near-demoniac frenzy of the all-too-human consequences of civic strife. The speech in question is Cicero's defense of Aulus Cluentius Habitus, a well-to-do resident of the Italian town of Larinum, who is charged with having bribed a jury in a previous trial to return a wrongful conviction against a fellow townsman. The case is both superficially complex and at heart very simple. If we reconstruct the social structure at Larinum we can see that in the decade before the trial of Cluentius the town had four or five leading families. Through a variety of events – deaths, divorces, marriages – Cluentius' mother Sassia and her new husband, Oppianicus (whose conviction Cluentius is charged with having obtained wrongly), have gained control of the estates of all but the Cluentii – and even that they hold in part. Thus, if we set aside Cicero's interpretation of motives and largely unsubstantiated account of particular events, we are left with a rather straightforward fight over property, and to a lesser extent, social dominance in a small town. Cicero's main strategy in the case is to suggest that Oppianicus, in cahoots with Sassia, was so obviously guilty of the crimes he was charged with that Cluentius had no need to bribe the previous jury. But the specific accusations he makes against the dead Oppianicus and the very much alive Sassia are precisely those that historians and anthropologists have taught us to expect when transfers of property destabilize a small community: namely, false wills, seductions, and poisonings. Such accusations, even if they fail to alter the transfer of property, nonetheless diminish the social status of the beneficiaries of a windfall. A reduction in symbolic capital balances an increase in material assets.

In a sense, then, the whole situation at Larinum looks a little bit like a contemporary soap opera, or a small-town melodrama, but with one difference: parties to events at Larinum become entangled in the larger affairs of Rome and Italy. And this entanglement is what transforms the case from local farce to large-scale tragedy. For example, we learn that the son of one of the leading families in Larinum was captured in the Marsian War (a struggle between Rome and a perennially independent-minded Italic people) and ended up as the slave of a Roman senator. When members of the young man's family publicly accuse Oppianicus of interfering with their efforts to ransom him, Oppianicus eludes them by joining the Roman forces of Sulla. When the latter seize control of Larinum, in one of the military actions of the Social Wars, Oppianicus sees to it that all the leading members of the Aurian clan are proscribed and executed. It should be noted that events of this sort, as opposed to seductions and poisonings, would have been easily verifiable by either side in the case. So, too, would have been Cluentius' own attempt to drag the power of Rome into the local conflict, by pursuing Oppianicus in court at Rome, eight years earlier; so too, the attempt on the part of Oppianicus' surviving son, who turns out to be the prosecutor in the present case, to destroy Cluentius, again by invoking the power of a Roman court.

For all that Cicero presents the case as being about the personal wickedness of Oppianicus and Sassia, and the personal reliability of "his good friend" Aulus Cluentius Habitus, it is also a reflection of the ways in which the Social Wars, proscriptions, and political disruptions of the preceding decades had torn apart the fabric of Italian life, even to the point of pitting family members against one another and creating startling reversals of fortune for individuals who managed to survive the turmoil.

The historical and social dimensions of the case, which are never addressed explicitly by Cicero, find their outlet in his virulent attack on the character of Cluentius' mother – and Oppianicus' widow – Sassia. Sassia appears as a villainess motivated by nothing other than wickedness almost from the outset of the speech. Of the marriage that produced the defendant, Cicero states "it was proceeding in a respectable and harmonious manner, when suddenly there boiled up the unspeakable lust of that unbearable woman, her passion ready for any action, no matter how repulsive or vile" (*In Defense of Cluentius* 12). This unmotivated wickedness on the part of Sassia figures in almost every aspect of the subsequent narrative: it is she who seduces, poisons, plots – and gloats at the success of her machinations. The speech is a long one, and during the stretches that describe the ins and outs of the trial of Oppianicus Cicero almost loses sight of Sassia. But this is because he wants to train his rhetorical guns on her at the finale, in a misogynistic rhetorical assault scarcely matched in the long history of classical poetry and prose. Not only has Sassia seduced her son-in-law and plotted against various relatives: it turns out, according to Cicero, that it is she who killed Oppianicus, and she who even tried to poison the defendant Cluentius! When that attempt failed, she put Oppianicus' son up to the judicial attack on Cluentius, and feverishly made her way to Rome to see to it that the attack succeeded:

> And just what do you suppose her journey to Rome was like? Can't you imagine . . . the crowds in the towns along the way? the groans that issued from men and women alike? Can't you just picture this female rushing from Larinum all the way to Rome, with an enormous retinue – not to mention a huge sum of money, all the better to attack and crush her own son by accusing him of a capital crime! Everyone she passed along the way felt certain that the very ground she touched was in need of ritual purification; that the earth itself, mother of us all, was being violated by the footsteps of a mother so wicked, so depraved!
> (*In Defense of Cluentius* 192–3)

But Cicero has not quite finished. He calls upon all the men of Larinum and neighboring towns who have also traveled to Rome, but in support of Cluentius, to stand up and be counted, and he tells us that tears are flowing from their cheeks as they contemplate the fate of Cluentius if the jury does not save him from his mother.

> And what a mother she is! ... Never has any fear of dishonor restrained her lust. Her viciousness runs roughshod over the laws of humanity . . . The very terms used to define human relationships, not to mention the very laws of nature, she transforms, becoming wife of her son-in-law, stepmother of her son, mistress to the husband of her daughter! (*In Defense of Cluentius* 199)

It is a timeworn rhetorical strategy to create solidarity within a fragmented group by pinning the blame for all troubles on a scapegoat. But of course the scapegoat is only an externalized manifestation of what the excluding community finds unacceptable about itself. And so Sassia becomes much more than a red herring or distraction for the jury as they ponder Cluentius' guilt or innocence. Rather, she becomes the personification of all the ways in which they, as Romans and Italians, senators and knights, soldiers and civilians, have "transformed the very terms used to define human relationships" during the previous decades of civil strife. Here, as elsewhere, Cicero taps into emotions and experiences that are made to seem beyond analysis. He draws upon and contributes to traditions of male blame of women. But the particular charges he lays against Sassia are the ones that he and his audience cannot, but somehow must, lay against themselves. As with his invocation of the gods as sacrificial avengers, his summoning of the ghosts of Clodius and others, his personification of the laws, his impersonation of friends and enemies alike, so here, with his materialization of guilt over civil strife, Cicero exemplifies the orator's social function as intermediary between the here and now and the world beyond everyday perception.

With the rise of the Roman principate, opportunities for achieving glory through oratory diminished. Defendants still required patrons, and public officials still deliberated on matters of importance, but the orator's role as sacred representative of the community was replaced by that of the emperor. Yet it is interesting to note that the ancient biographies of emperors still make much of their successes or failures as public speakers. Indeed, mastery of oratory, associated as it was with deliberation, analysis, respect for the audience, and acknowledgment of the history and procedures of the state, serves as a mark of a "good" emperor in the eyes of the Roman elite; disdain for eloquence, on the other hand, signals unreliability and worse. We get a sense of how the figure of the orator shapes expectations and evaluations of an emperor from the imperial historians' account of Nero's habits of public performance. As Tacitus tells it, Nero was educated by Seneca the Younger, himself an orator, philosopher, and playwright of some renown. Yet when Nero, as first public act of his new reign, delivered the funeral oration for his stepfather, the emperor Claudius, it somehow became known that the speech had been written not by Nero but by Seneca. This was a first for an emperor, as Tacitus has old folks in the audience note. And it was a radical rupture in another respect as well. One of the oldest traditions of the Roman aristocracy had been for a young member of the clan to make his public debut by delivering the eulogy for a recently deceased member of the family. Even in Tacitus' day, it would seem, the tradition had been at most revised, not abandoned, as young men made their entry into public life through recitation of some text they had composed.

In the case of Nero, the abandonment of aristocratic and dynastic traditions of self-presentation through language is a harbinger of more severe changes to come. As is well known, Nero comes to seek glory outside the realm of eloquence. He races chariots, he enters singing competitions, he performs passages from epic poetry and tragedy. In other words, Nero acknowledges the performative dimensions of the old traditions, but disavows the elements of deliberation, analysis, and respectful presentation of the self for the scrutiny of others that also characterized those traditions at their best. Far from it, Tacitus tells us that the judges in the competitions Nero did enter were too frightened to offer him anything but first prize. Once again, we can read such anecdotes as morality tales, somewhat as Cicero wants us to interpret the cruelty of Sassia; or we can see them as the ancient writers' way of exploring societal issues and problems through concrete examples. In the case of Nero, the issues implied in the anecdotes include the proper comportment of the emperor, the need for strategies of communication to reach ever-expanding audiences, the triangular relation among the emperor, the educated elite, and the masses of the population, and, ultimately, the ongoing transformation of Rome from city-state into a radically different political and cultural system.

As I suggested earlier, the state needs to get control of its dead. By establishing a clear boundary between the dead and the living, it creates the possibility of history, that is, of the orderly transition from one generation to the next within a recognizably continuous social framework. To the extent that rhetoric is the discourse of the state, it is also a discourse of control over and access to the dead. We have seen this relationship exemplified in different ways by Pericles, Demosthenes, and most especially Cicero. By highlighting Nero's inability to deliver a funeral oration on his own, Tacitus calls attention to the transformations that are underway. Not, I submit, a straightforward transformation between republic and principate: for Tacitus accepts the possibility of an emperor who can speak competently on his own, about the dead as well as the living. But Nero's reign marked the end of the Julio-Claudian dynasty, a collapse that led to yet another round of wildly destructive civil war. Rome recovered, and a succession of emperors of varying temperament and caliber followed. Now, in Tacitus' own day, indeed, near the end of his days, since his work on Nero was the last work he wrote, a new emperor, Hadrian, has taken power. And, as the Roman historian Ronald Syme has noted, Hadrian had more than a little of Nero about him, especially in his universalizing cultural ambitions.[2] Tacitus thus seems to use the experience of Nero, in particular his turn away from rhetoric and oratory, as a way of reflecting on, and perhaps influencing, what was going on around him.

As it turned out, the Roman state, and the traditions of Greek and Roman rhetoric that informed it, was more resilient than Tacitus may have feared. Plenty of later emperors were skilled speakers, and plenty of skilled speakers who never became emperors flourished throughout the later empire. But the way Tacitus expresses his fears, or those of his contemporaries, in an account of the failure, or better, abandonment of rhetoric on the part of the princeps, is testimony to his own understanding of the deep connection between rhetoric and the state and of the complex role of the orator in fashioning the state from within. His implicit warning, that the neglect of rhetoric and dishonoring of the orator foretell profound social and political convulsions, speaks to later ages as well.

3

The Craft of Rhetoric

Early in the fourth century BC rhetoric came to be identified as a craft, or in Greek, *tekhnê*. The term was not necessarily intended as a compliment, since craftsmanship was regarded as socially and epistemologically subordinate to the comprehensive knowledge of the well-born. The work that rhetores and their collaborators had done to regularize processes of speechmaking was grudgingly acknowledged as just that – work. The philosopher Plato gives away the game of social one-upmanship when, at the end of the *Phaedrus*, he has Socrates praise the "better-born" Isocrates as purveyor of rhetorical studies at the expense of the metic, or resident alien, Lysias, who seems to have turned to speechwriting after his family lost its fortune during the oligarchical revolution at Athens in 403 BC.

Plato's Socrates subjects the speechwriting craft of Lysias to withering critique by analyzing a speech allegedly written by him and delivered, at the outset of the *Phaedrus*, by Phaedrus himself, who turns out to be Lysias' lover. The speech is something of a joke, inasmuch as it is an attempt to persuade a youth to submit to the advances not of his lover but of one who does not love him. Phaedrus delivers the gist of the speech from memory, even though he has a written copy hidden beneath his cloak. The paradoxical nature of the speech, which is only intensified through its delivery by one of a pair of lovers, the seemingly unnecessary reliance on memorization when the written script is available, and the absence of the author Lysias, whose words nonetheless catalyze the entire dialogue – all of these features remind Plato's reader of Lysias' status as a logographos, that is, a writer of speeches to be delivered by others. While Socrates has some fairly interesting philosophical reasons for rejecting both the content and the craft of Lysias' oration, we should not overlook the fact that he is a freeborn citizen passing judgment on the achievement of a man who, due to his non-citizen status, is excluded from participating directly in either judicial or deliberative processes.

Socrates' snub of Lysias, matched by his condescending attitude toward the non-citizen Gorgias in the dialogue of the same name, is its own argument against the spread of the craft of rhetoric. As a craft, that is to say, a teachable skill, rhetoric is not tied to the bloodlines of the citizen body. Born in Sicily, as we saw in chapter 1, transplanted to Athens by the migrant Gorgias, who among other problems taught for pay, and in subsequent years practiced successfully by the metic Lysias, rhetoric is a dangerously non-native, non-aristocratic discourse. It is a bastard art, in danger of corrupting (if it hasn't already done so) the flower of Athenian citizenry, from the intemperate Callicles of the *Gorgias* to the more accommodating Phaedrus. The social critique of rhetoric thus dovetails with the philosophical, which one scholar has summarized as the objection that in the case of speechmaking the writer and speaker seek persuasion while the audience seeks truth, whereas in the case of philosophical inquiry, all parties have the same aim.[1] But isn't a difference in goals precisely what we would expect when one party is an outsider, the other an Athenian?

It is thus far from accidental that the success of Lysias is the jumping-off point for the Socratic critique of rhetoric. But that same success just as easily serves as evidence of the power of rhetoric as craft, a power independent of the charisma of the orator. And indeed such craftsmanship – and power – are well attested in the corpus of surviving speeches attributed to Lysias and to other logographoi as well. If the charismatic orators discussed in the preceding chapter represent the heights to which rhetoric might aspire, workhorses like Lysias and his successors help us to appreciate its pervasiveness.

To take but two small examples, we may consider the third and seventh of the surviving Lysian orations. Speech No. 3 shows an interesting overlap in content with the alleged speech of Lysias in Plato's *Phaedrus*. In the case in question, an unnamed speaker defends himself against the charge of having assaulted one Simon with intent to kill. Because of the nature of the charge, the case is being tried before the Council of the Areopagus, whose membership is dominated by the conservative, landowning aristocracy. The speaker, using words composed by Lysias, represents himself as the aggrieved party. As he tells the story, it is because Simon lusted after the speaker's young

male companion, a Plataean youth named Theodotus, that he harassed
both the speaker and the youth, breaking into the house they shared,
throwing stones, even organizing a party to kidnap Theodotus. To
the obvious objection that the speaker should have pressed charges
against Simon instead of waiting to be hauled into court himself, the
speaker offers different answers at different points in his oration: he
was embarrassed by the nature of his own relationship with Theodotus
(Lysias 3.3–4); he feared that irresponsible citizens would laugh at
him for attempting to enforce a traditional code of conduct (Lysias
3.9); he thought the consequences of a guilty verdict against Simon,
namely exile and confiscation, would be unnecessarily harsh for
misbehavior arising from a quarrel over a boy (Lysias 3.40). What at
first glance might appear as signs of inconsistency or befuddlement
on the part of the speaker in fact position him quite specifically with
respect to the composition of his audience. Even in the fourth century
BC, pederasty, or ritualized courtship between an adult male and a
youth, was considered a socially elite practice. Exposure of the speaker's
intimate relationship with Theodotus is thus unlikely to embarrass
him before his immediate audience. What might have embarrassed
him would be to use the relationship as a basis for first-strike legal
action against Simon, with the requisite gathering of witnesses, evidence, and the like. The relationship with Theodotus, far from being
prejudicial to the case, may well strengthen the bond between speaker
and jury at the expense of the plaintiff. The speaker's delicate handling
of the matter only confirms this impression. Moreover, litigiousness
itself figures in Athenian discourse as a sign of democratic, as opposed
to aristocratic, affiliations. The speaker's admission that he could have,
but didn't, bring a case against Simon further identifies him with the
jury at the expense of the plaintiff. When the speaker refers to those
"who are habitually envious of anyone who is eager to behave responsibly in the city" (Lysias 3.9), he might just as well be inviting the
jury to reflect on the difficulties they face and have faced in carrying
out their own responsibilities, both in court and beyond. The speaker
presents himself as closer in social status to the jury than to the
plaintiff. This is not necessarily to say that he expects the jury to vote
in his favor out of class allegiance, only that the character he presents
is one he expects the audience to find familiar and reassuring.

The speaker of Lysias 3 gives further evidence of his social and
personal status through the very structure of his presentation. The
organization of the speech exactly follows the guidelines set down in

later rhetorical handbooks. The speech commences with an introductory appeal to the jury, one designed to secure their goodwill: as the
speaker puts it, "If others were about to pass judgment on me, I
would be very anxious about facing trial . . . but since I am appearing
before you, I fully anticipate a fair outcome" (Lysias 3.2). After this
brief proem, the speech proceeds to a simple but detailed chronological
narrative of the events in question (*diêgêsis* in Greek, *narratio* in
Latin). This narration culminates in an explicit statement of contrast
between the positions of the disputants, followed by a refutation
(Greek *lysis*, Latin *refutatio*) of the opponent's account, here described
as "the lies he has told" (Lysias 3.22). After again summarizing the
key points of the case, the speaker turns the remaining issues of the
case – here the aim of the law under which he is being tried and
the nature of his opponent's character – into argumentation in his
favor (Greek *pistis*, Latin *argumentatio*). Although not strictly relevant,
the latter argument in particular continues the speaker's effort to
distance the plaintiff from the jurors. He goes so far as to suggest
that the very fact of the prosecution removes the plaintiff from
the category of those who are "simple" (Greek *euêthês*) in nature –
an expression that is something of a codeword for aristocratic
self-presentation. In contrast, he reminds his audience, he himself
has "performed many liturgies" for Athens, and comes from a long-
established family that had done no harm to the fatherland: exactly
the sort of emotional and, we might add, political appeal recommended
by the handbooks as appropriate for the summary, or peroration
(Greek *epilogos*, Latin *peroratio*) of the case.

    Although no surviving rhetorical handbooks are securely datable to
the period before Lysias' prime, we have good reason to believe such
treatises existed. Plato alludes to them in the *Phaedrus* when he has
the title character mention *tekhnai peri logôn* written by Gorgias,
Thrasymachus, and Theodorus (*Phaedrus* 261c), and he seems to
signal awareness of their content when he has Socrates analyze Lysias'
speech for its invention (*heuresis*) and arrangement (*diathesis*, 236a),
and refers to Phaedrus' attempt at memorization (*apomnêmoneusein*,
228a): in effect, three of the five traditional subdivisions of the
rhetorical art (the other two being delivery and style). Lysias' employ-
ment, in the speech against Simon, of the canonical parts of a speech,
in the most commonly recommended order, might be understood
as the fountainhead of a long tradition. But it is more likely that he
has his speaker reflect established practice, not only to give his speech

an orderly presentation for its own sake, but also as a manifestation of his ethos as a well-to-do educated citizen. Indeed, the speaker of Lysias 3 is almost too good to be true: educated and intelligent, an adherent to traditional aristocratic practices, one capable of coming to the aid of the city, but unlikely to waste its time on trivialities or to expose the aristocratic lifestyle to demotic ridicule. In what is, as so often in ancient legal cases, a debate over inclusion or exclusion, exile or retention of citizen rights, it is hard to see how he could lose, regardless of the mundane details of the case.

The speaker of Lysias 7 also faces loss of property and citizenship rights, in his case on the grounds that he had destroyed a *sêkos*, probably to be understood as the stump of a sacred olive tree. Since there is apparently no evidence – the prosecution alleges that the speaker had the wood hauled off – the speaker is in the difficult position of having to prove a negative: there never was a *sêkos* on the estate in question, and so there was no sacrilege against it. His argument proceeds less through an orderly narrative than through a series of challenges to the plaintiff: why didn't you produce a witness to the pre-existence of the *sêkos* or to the alleged crime itself? Isn't it possible the (non-existent) *sêkos* was destroyed during the long war with Sparta or by previous tenants of the estate? Why would I have destroyed this *sêkos* on this estate when there are many sacred olive trees on other estates I own, where the disappearance of one would have been less noticeable? And why do you suggest that I removed the *sêkos* in broad daylight? Given the seriousness of the punishment against such an act, wouldn't I have performed it at a time when I was more likely to avoid detection? Finally, why didn't you accept my offer to have my slaves give evidence under torture?

It is in many ways a peculiar speech. If indeed the plaintiff had failed to present witnesses, as the speaker suggests, and failed to document the existence of a *sêkos* in the first place, why not just point out those omissions and be done with it? Part of the answer must reside in the speaker's need to convey a sense of his own character as worthy of inclusion in the citizen body. He needs to make clear that he is wealthy without having oligarchic tendencies, that he has fulfilled his responsibilities to the state without overstepping his bounds. As for display of rhetorical competence, this he achieves not through the structure of his speech, which is rather chaotic, but through his implied instruction of his opponent in the way he ought to have organized his own speech. Unlike speaker 3, who evinces familiarity with the rules of disposition of an orderly speech, speaker 7 is something of an aficionado of invention: the questions and challenges he poses to his opponent resemble the structured brainstorming sessions that handbooks recommend as part of the process of developing an argument in response to the specifics of the matter under consideration. This speech, like Speech 3, thus displays two levels of craftsmanship: Lysias' craft in tailoring language and argument to project the appropriate character for the circumstances and the speaker's display, as part of that projected craft, of just enough rhetorical skill to count among those worth listening to and believing.

What seems to bother Socrates about all of this is not just that such craftsmanship can be purchased, and from an outsider, but also that it proceeds from no clear basis in a preexistent reality. Neither speaker begins with a definition of terms, as Socrates insists all good speeches must, nor can we tell, from the speeches alone, what really happened. Moreover, the suppleness of Lysias' rhetoric prompts an anxiety over the source of difference between the speakers: is it generated by a true difference in identity or by Lysias' responsiveness to the particulars of each rhetorical situation? Socrates and his followers don't so much deny the power of rhetorical speech as fear it. Through its craftsmanship rhetoric is being transformed from communication with the world beyond into a means of fashioning the world and the human subjects that populate it.

Of course, rhetoric's potential to alter the world is precisely what prompts its proliferation. Philosophers will try to tame the power of the craft by subjugating it to or basing it on their own (self-proclaimed) comprehensive and foundational knowledge. But this tactic – deployed most aggressively in Aristotle's *Rhetoric* – speaks more to the philosopher's desire to remain functional within the ancient city-state than to any deep commitment to the rhetorical enterprise. Indeed, the particular contribution for which Aristotelian rhetoric is most often cited by modern admirers – his emphasis on the need to understand human psychology – is actually a retreat from the rhetorical position that would see human subjectivity as constituted through language, not preexisting "out there" waiting to be "discovered" by the student of philosophical rhetoric. Plato's critique and Aristotle's response to it, for all their influence on the post-classical world, have little or no impact on the lived processes of making, analyzing, and remaking persuasive speech in the classical world. Despite occasional references to the educational value and literary grandeur of Plato and

Aristotle, purveyors of rhetoric remain unimpressed by their efforts to contain the impact of rhetoric as a craft. Indeed, they end up turning the irony of Socrates and the analytical power of Aristotle into resources for their own enterprise.

And quite an enterprise it is, for the rhetorical handbook, often entitled *tekhnê rhêtorikê* or *ars rhetorica*, is quite possibly the single best-attested genre of writing from the ancient world. We have reference to at least four or five tekhnai prior to Plato (Socrates even jokes that Nestor and Odysseus were probably writing *tekhnai rhêtorikai* in their spare time at Troy: *Phaedrus* 261c). There are major discussions in the mid-fourth century BC by Isocrates and Aristotle. Aristotle's association with Alexander may be what prompts dedication of a slightly later, and more assertively practical, tekhne to the world-conqueror (this is the so-called *Rhetoric for Alexander*). The Hellenistic period sees successive waves of rhetorical treatises or handbooks, some apparently prompted by a desire to peddle old educational wares to new Roman masters. And the Romans themselves do not fail to get in on the act: the anonymous author of the *Rhetoric for Herennius* implies that he is not the first to adapt Greek rhetorical teaching to Roman contexts and examples. Cicero cuts his rhetorical teeth with a youthful treatise *On Invention* (or the means of finding the right argument for each section of a speech) and incorporates extensive technical discussion in his later, more wide-ranging reflections on the social role of oratory (i.e., *De Oratore* and *Orator*), as well as dealing with circumscribed aspects of rhetorical craft in two shorter works, *Partitiones oratoriae* and *Topica*. The writing of treatises continued unabated after Cicero's murder; indeed, it seems to have received new impetus therefrom. And so widespread is the teaching of rhetoric that in the late first century AD the Roman writer Quintilian, holder of what was in effect an endowed chair in rhetoric at Rome, produces not an ars but a guidebook for the teachers of the ars of rhetoric, the twelve-volume *Institutio Oratoria*.

Meanwhile, Greek writers under the Roman empire were not to be outdone. A wide range of writers from throughout the empire and from varying philosophical (or aphilosophical) perspectives made their contributions. Best known among these is Hermogenes of Tarsus, a writer of the second century AD to whom works on *Issues* (or, as it is often called, status theory: see below), on *Types of Style*, on *Invention*, and on *How to Achieve Awesomeness in Style*, as well as a set of preliminary exercises known as *Progymnasmata*, are attributed.

Hermogenes preserves certain aspects of rhetorical lore that we might not know of otherwise. Yet even his seemingly original contributions can be understood as elaborations or variations on themes rung by earlier writers: his work *On Issues* owes much to the lost treatment centuries earlier by Hermagoras, as demonstrated by overlap with other writers, such as Quintilian; and his discussion of *Types of Style* echoes treatises by Theophrastus and Dionysius of Halicarnassus, as well as a roughly contemporary study attributed to Aelius Aristides. What is more, the process of repeated subdivision of broad issues into narrower and narrower topics that characterizes *On Issues* recalls the organization of the early fragmentary discussions of rhetoric by the great sophists of Periclean Athens. Once set in motion, the proliferation of treatises is effectively unstoppable. Indeed, subsequent to the rediscovery of Hermogenes by Western Europeans in the Renaissance, at least sixteen editions and translations of *On Issues* appear within a period of about 150 years.

This multiplication of handbooks suggests that something else is at stake besides devotion to the growth of rhetorical knowledge. One version of status theory is quite enough, since the whole point is not to be comprehensive but to prod the student into finding the most appropriate means of persuasion. And while it is hard for us to see how it matters whether the examples of particular points a rhetorician supplies have been located by him in others' speeches and poems or invented to serve as illustration, the author of the *Rhetoric for Herennius* was quite sure it did, and boasted aggressively about his own prowess in the latter technique. The distinct impression left by the surviving treatises is that the production of a tekhne or ars is itself a kind of rhetorical performance, a demonstration of mastery either on the part of a pupil seeking to enter the ranks of practitioner (e.g., Cicero with *De Inventione*) or on the part of a teacher trawling for pupils. The ars is thus the equivalent to the "masterpiece" of later schools of painting or the "master-song" (*Meistergesang*) of the late medieval musical tradition. And as is often the case in the production of artistic masterpieces, the craftsman demonstrates his mastery of the traditions of the craft by producing something that is just different enough from its predecessors to be distinctive without, by its difference, implying criticism of what preceded (the so-called "principle of least difference"). We might see a contemporary parallel to the multiplication of rhetorical treatises in the proliferation of self-help or business how-to manuals – often recycling the same material in slightly different form. These latterday treatises, too, seek to establish the mastery of the author (indeed, are often connected with expensive seminars) while also speaking to the insecurity of the reader in an endlessly competitive business or social environment.

The repetition, adaptation, and reuse of rhetorical lore in no way suggests that the ancient tekhnai or artes are without use, or that all treatises are variations on the same theme. In fact, there seem to be two distinct if overlapping traditions of treatise, one jumping right into the technical details, reveling in the ins and outs of thesis and hypothesis, finite versus infinite topics, issues of conjecture, definition, logic, practice, and transference, anadiplosis and anacephaleosis, isocolon, tricolon, apostrophe and paronomasia, the three levels of style versus the seven types or the however many virtues, and so on; the other apologizing, justifying, rationalizing – before reveling in the ins and outs of same. The difference is significant and seems to speak to a difference in political and, ultimately, epistemological framework traceable to the birth of rhetoric as a craft alongside of philosophy in the context of the Athenian democracy: on the one hand, the sophists, whose rhetoric threatens to destabilize traditional authority within the polis, in part by showing that there are two sides to every issue; on the other hand, Plato, whose quest to restabilize the polis can only succeed if rhetoric is given a minor and subordinate role.

Which is not to say that there is a simple equation between philosophical approaches and oligarchy, on the one hand, and a more technical approach and democracy, on the other, as has sometimes been implied. The anonymous author of the *Rhetoric for Alexander* writes a straightforward and probably rather effective technical treatise, one that gives suggestions for how to argue a case differently in a democracy versus an oligarchy. But he prefaces the treatise with an unctuous dedication to Alexander the Great, lauding him for replacing democracy with one-man rule. On the other hand, the Roman author of the treatise for Herennius, another workmanlike work that expressly eschews "irrelevancy," and one that incorporates a veritable anti-optimate political platform in its fictitious examples, nevertheless describes his work on rhetoric as a distraction from the serious business of philosophy. Cicero, in turn, reverses the relationship between business and leisure, suggesting that the business of the forum (i.e., speechmaking) is the only serious enterprise, with the writing of both rhetorical and philosophical treatises a type of compensation when leisure has been forced upon him by political circumstances beyond his control. What is more, for all that he seems to share the Platonic preference for stability and suspicion of democracy, Cicero, more than any other ancient writer, makes the case for the comprehensiveness, indeed the sufficiency, of rhetorical knowledge. He asserts exactly what Socrates denies, namely that the orator is in effect master of all he purveys, that his craft encompasses the craft even of philosophy. If the rhetorical handbooks, then, do not fall into neat political categories, nonetheless it seems clear that the work they do is never apolitical. Talking, writing, and teaching about the language of the state cannot help having political implications, then or now.

What exactly did the handbooks teach? We have already made reference to the canonical division of rhetoric into five parts – invention, disposition, style, memory, and performance; the categorization of speeches as deliberative, judicial, or demonstrative; and the subdivision of the standard judicial speech into proem, narrative, division, refutation, argumentation, and peroration. Add to these the three goals of rhetoric (to teach, to move, to persuade), the need to match style, argument, performance, etc. to audience and situation (the doctrine of decorum), as well as meta-questions of the appropriate means of educating the orator in all of the above and of the ultimate role of oratory and rhetoric in society and you have a collective table of contents of the rhetorical treatises taken as a whole. In order to get a sense of how these treatises approach their material, let us examine here a little more closely two of the more complex "parts" of rhetoric, namely invention, or the finding of arguments within the material, and style, or the rendering of argument in language. Yet another part of rhetoric, performance, will be considered in chapter 4 on the role of rhetoric in the acculturation of youth and outsiders.

To find an argument implies that the matter of rhetoric is preexistent. Hence, the standard English expression "invention" is a bit misleading, since it can wrongly connote imagination or fictionalizing. The ancient rhetorician does not make things up, he takes them out – of the evidence, the witnesses, the defense, the expectations of the community. Aristotle writes of *pisteis*, proofs, or more accurately, things that generate belief or confidence, but later writers saw that it was impossible to speak of generating belief or confidence until one had a sense of what one was to generate belief or confidence in. Hence, the teaching of invention came to prioritize careful analysis of the issue at hand. Is it a matter of the truth or falsity of a specific claim, the

applicability of the law, the interpretation of the act in question, or of
the law in question? Does the dispute concern a past action or a
possible future action? If past, is it possible that someone besides
the defendant was responsible for it? If the defendant accepts responsibility, are there mitigating factors? What would the consequences
have been if the parties involved had not acted as they are said to have
acted? Does the letter of the law correspond to its intent? Does the
case hinge upon possible ambiguity in the law?

Notice how investigation of these so-called "issues" or "statuses"
(better: stances?) forces the speaker to probe more deeply into the
matter at hand. Once he has identified the issue or issues of the case,
he must ascertain how to present it. Here the proofs of which Aristotle
and others write come into play: so-called atechnic or artless proofs,
such as testimony and documents, as well as technical, or crafted
proofs, derived, according to Aristotle, from character (ethos), emotion (pathos), and rational use of language (logos). But how to find
the right proofs among or within the various possibilities? Here again,
Aristotle is less helpful, simply discussing the legitimacy of each pistis.
Later rhetoricians fill in the gap, developing a system of places (Greek
topoi, Latin *loci*) within the matter (Greek *hylê*, Latin *res*) where likely
arguments and approaches are to be found. The investigation of topoi
is much too complicated to be summarized here. It encompasses a
search into person and matter, with subdivisions pertaining to place,
time, manner, capacity, definition, etc. It also invites the speaker to
move outward from the case into the general understanding of the
community. This is because each specific topos or locus can be linked
to a more common one, the so-called *loci communes* that come to
assume an important role not just in rhetoric and oratory but in
poetry and philosophy as well. For example, attack on the credibility
of a particular witness can lead to more generalized reflections on the
credibility (or not) of witnesses as a class. An expression of sympathy
for the sufferings of the victim invites elaboration on victimization as
a general phenomenon or on the special vulnerability of the particular
group to which the victim belongs. The *loci communes* are an important
type of argument because they relate the details of the case, in which
the audience may have no particular involvement, to situations with
which they might be familiar. They also give the speaker an easy means
to amplify his case, making it (and him) seem grander, more significant
than they may in fact be. Finally, since the *loci communes* are, as their
name suggests, common, and, some rhetoricians suggest, boundless

in relevance, they can be used over and over again in different speeches on different subjects.

To the modern reader or listener, the insertion of commonplaces in a speech might convey a sense of falsehood or insincerity. Who wants to hear a prosecutor or a politician drone on about "times like these" (*locus de saeculo*), the dangers of the inner city (*locus de loco*), and so on? To the ancients, they apparently had the opposite effect, anchoring the details of the case in a more broadly acceptable and shared worldview. The process of invention thus requires the speaker to extract arguments from the matter before him, then relate them to more general themes and topics. His role in this respect is the inverse of that of the singer of earlier times. The singer brings order to chaos through the ritualization of language and imagery. As some would put it, he imposes form on matter. In one sense, simply by employing formal speech, the rhetorician engages in the same process. But in the development of his case, he locates the form preexistent in the matter, then transforms it into something more generally recognizable.

This transformative role of the rhetor becomes especially clear when we move from the realm of invention to that of style. The Latin word for style, *elocutio*, is suggestive in this regard. The Latin prefix *e-*, as recent scholarship has shown, describes a transformation from one state to another. To evacuate a city is not to empty it out, but to transform its state from full to empty. To elucidate a subject is to bring it from a state of obscurity to a state of visibility. So, too, to participate in *elocutio* is to transform *res* from unspoken, unvoiced, to spoken. This sense of transformation into or even creation of a new state is important for understanding ancient notions of style. Too often, modern scholars (myself included) have described style as a matter of choice, as if somehow the same meaning could be expressed in several different ways and still remain the same meaning. It is not at all clear that the ancients believed such a feat was possible. When they do speak of the rearrangement of words, it is to emphasize the transformation of effect, for better or for worse, that such rearrangement generates. But rearrangement is only a minuscule part of their discussions of style anyway. For the ancient rhetoricians, style is the creation or crafting of a verbal artifact. Like all crafting, it effects a transformation. It is through style that the rhetorician reclaims the authority of the magician. In effect, he is a conjurer, making something exist that was not there before. This sense of the creative power of the speaker propels the continuing interest in style in antiquity and helps to explain its declining importance today. Just as regard for style empowers the speaker of old, makes of him a conduit between the mysteries of reality and the mind of the community, so too disregard for style today is the sign of the modern speaker's disrespect for himself, his audience, or both.

The rhetorically trained speaker's potential for linguistic creativity is virtually infinite. If discussion of invention tends to generate a set of strategies for finding the most appropriate stance and argument, in essence, for limiting the speaker's set of arguments, the handbook treatments of style struggle to categorize and transmit the limitless possibilities of language. Lists of figures of thought and figures of speech grow ever longer; examples abound; nuances proliferate. Immediately striking to the modern reader is the extraordinary amount of energy devoted to the study and teaching of style. Thus, the magisterial modern compendium of ancient and medieval literary rhetoric by the German scholar Heinrich Lausberg devotes 95 pages to invention, 6 pages to disposition, 263 to style, 2 to memory, and 1 to delivery. Since Lausberg's focus is literary rhetoric, we can understand his neglect of memory and delivery (understand but not approve, since performance has always been an important part of literature as well as rhetoric). Nonetheless, his ratio of the other parts seems to get things about right. What is more, when we consider the ancient treatises chronologically, an increase in the relative attention to style becomes apparent. Aristotle covers *lexis* in half a book out of a three-book treatise. The author of the *Rhetorica ad Herennium* devotes an entire book out of four. Cicero, who expands the range of the rhetorical treatise to take in broader political and moral questions, nonetheless devotes a third of the *De Oratore* to style, and a significant portion of a separate work, *Orator*, to a particular aspect of style, namely the use of rhythmical endings, or clausulae, for sentences and sentence subdivisions. Roughly a third as well of Quintilian's *Institutio Oratoria* addresses style, with the proportion becoming significantly greater if we exclude his first book on child psychology and his last, a meditation on the social relationship between philosophy and oratory. Finally, Hermogenes manages to cover issue theory in 64 pages of dense Greek prose, but devotes 200 pages to his treatise *Types of Style* – a number that becomes even more impressive if we append the possibly pseudonymous 42-page treatise on *How to Achieve Awesomeness in Style*.

This obsession with style and all of its subcomponents – choice of vocabulary, word order, sentence length, paragraph structure, euphony and sound effects, thought-figures (e.g., metaphor and metonymy), rhythm, decorum, imagery, personification, emphasis, amplification, dramatization, and so on – exactly illustrates the paradoxical political and social status of rhetoric in the ancient world touched on briefly in the first chapter of this book. On the one hand, mastery of style allows the speaker to create the world anew, to bring into language characters, ideas, situations, beliefs, and practices that would otherwise be the purview of the possessors of occult or mystical knowledge. This generative aspect of style is apparent in the very terms Hermogenes applies to the types or ideals of style: clarity (sapheneia), bulk (megethos), beauty (kallos), speed (gorgotes), character (ethos), unforgettability (aletheia), and awesomeness (deinotes). These terms are clearly more applicable to an animate being or a mimetic performance than to letters on a page. What is more, the sharing of this knowledge through handbooks and classroom teaching spreads this creative or generative power to larger and larger circles of the population. Even those who do not become important public speakers themselves are well positioned through rhetorical education to recognize the sleight-of-hand of those to whom they listen. This latter point becomes especially clear in the anecdotes of everyday life in the courtroom, the forum, the classroom, and the recitation hall told with such gusto by Seneca the Elder and Quintilian, wherein students, teachers, and competitors not only criticize speakers' infelicities but also deconstruct and reconstruct their premises and arguments.

At the same time, the more abstruse the lessons in style (or in any aspect of rhetoric), the less accessible they are to the common man (not to mention the common woman!). This latter point especially concerns Cicero, who wants to have his cake and eat it too. On the one hand, he revels in the crowd's appreciation of his and other orators' virtuosity. Take, for example, his claim that the crowd leapt to its feet when the orator Crassus concluded an important section of his speech with the metrical pattern known as the dichoree. "It was amazing how great a cry went up from the audience at this dichoree! I ask you wasn't it the rhythm that produced this effect? Change the order of the words . . . and nothing remains" (*Orator* 214). Indeed, what is the point of the elaborate training Cicero recommends if it doesn't have an impact on the average juror or voter? At the same time, Cicero is more than happy to set the stylistic bar higher and higher: thus, his insistence on urbanitas, or the speech of the city of Rome, as a stylistic virtue, a highly charged claim just a generation after non-Roman Italians fought a brutal war for inclusion in the Roman political, social, and economic system. Cicero's own attempt to negotiate between the shoals of vulgarity and elitism foundered, at least in the eyes of some of his younger rivals. They insisted on a purification of language, what came to be called Atticism, in contrast to the lusher, more inclusive style of Cicero, known as Asianism. Again, what might at first glance seem to be inert terms for esoteric rhetorical distinctions look different from the vantage point of a multicultural, multilingual empire struggling to redefine its culture. Style is in some ways the most political aspect of rhetoric precisely because it is the least open to direct political critique.

This chapter opened with consideration of two short speeches that illustrated the craft of rhetoric at an early phase of the rhetorical tradition. Indeed, my argument was that the virtuosity of Lysias may have prompted Socrates' application of the metaphor of craftsmanship to rhetoric. Two longer examples from late in the tradition give us some sense of how that tradition of craftsmanship persisted and, in particular, of how the orator/rhetorician as craftsman effects the transformation, even generation, of reality through mastery of language. The essential continuity between fifth and fourth century BC Athens, on the one hand, and second century AD Rome (and indeed we could find later illustrations, carrying our argument at least into fifth century Gaul and Byzantium) on the other, is an important point to consider. No matter how much the ancients seem to develop in the direction of modernity, no matter how complex their institutions and technologies, no matter how familiar they seem, there are always differences of outlook, different ways of conceptualizing language, nature, and human psychology that are difficult for the modern reader to grasp yet are of absolutely central importance if we are to view the ancients as anything other than a mirror of ourselves. In this context, anthropological studies of contemporary or recent societies that differ radically from the so-called First World societies of Europe and North America can sometimes point the way to a clearer understanding of the ancients. In trying to grasp the continuing force of ancient rhetoric as a craft, we might consider the remarks of anthropologist Mary Helms, who has studied the relationship between craftsmanship and social order in a wide array of societies, past and present. Helms calls attention to the variety of activities that can be construed as craft, such as carving, painting, weaving, singing, speechmaking, hunting, navigating. Already, we can see the close parallel with ancient Greek and Roman uses of the terms tekhne and ars. Helms further emphasizes the recurrent relationship between craftsmanship and access to a distant world. The connection with Greece and Rome is perhaps less obvious, but worth considering: we are reminded of the foreign origin of rhetoric, at least in the Greek foundation stories, but also of the way in which ancient rhetoric construes its subject matter as something obscure and enigmatic that requires careful scrutiny, exploration, and "discovery." Indeed, there would be nothing for orators to talk about if problems didn't arise that are outside the apprehension of everyday beliefs and practices. The orator is always dealing with something disruptive, whether he is advising on appropriate response to a miscreant foreign potentate (deliberation), taking sides in a dispute over alleged criminal activity (judicial speech), or trying to reconcile the dead and the living or the extraordinary and the everyday (speeches of eulogy, or of praise and blame).

Oratory, then, to follow Helms' analysis of craft, involves "the initial acquisition of some form of material from realms geographically or symbolically outside society . . . followed by their transformation into socially significant goods or public services."[2] Here again, the applicability of Helms' model to ancient rhetoric is precise, for after "finding" his approach, the rhetorician transforms the material into a socially significant linguistic artifact, namely a speech. The modern obsession with the truth or falsity of the relationship between the artifact (i.e., the speech) and the material (i.e., the facts of the case) is not by and large the concern of ancient rhetoric. It is not that the rhetorician has carte blanche to lie. Rather, society grants him a license to create. The truth he speaks is not the truth of empirical science but the truth of art. His goal is not to reflect but to create, and to create something socially significant, to cite Helms once again. Lysias' characterizations with which we opened this chapter are not to be judged for the accuracy of their portrayal of the speakers for whom they are designed (and anyway, how could we pass such judgment at this distance and given our ignorance of the men involved?); they are to be judged and evaluated for their social significance as verbal creations. Even Socrates, whose criticism of Lysias in certain ways anticipates the modern concern with empirically demonstrable truth, is ultimately just as interested in the social significance of oratory and rhetoric as the sophists, logographoi, and rhetoricians are. He just wants a greater degree of stability and predictability about the social outcome and perhaps, as I have suggested, tighter restrictions on who can practice the art of rhetoric.

Our reevaluation of the craft metaphor from the vantage point of anthropology helps us to understand the branch of rhetoric and oratory that is perhaps least accessible and least appealing to contemporary readers, namely the production of epideictic or eulogistic speeches. One type of eulogy, the funeral oration, is familiar, to be sure, but what of the grandiose laudations of subjects ranging from the ridiculous (e.g., salt, cabbage) to the (literally) sublime (e.g., gods, emperors, the city of Rome)? The point of such exercises seems to be not to capture or reflect a preexistent reality, but to create a kind of truth, an unforgettable and socially significant vision that in effect replaces the former, distant, imperceptible reality with a new, vivid, accessible one. The panegyrist doesn't describe salt; he creates salt as a socially significant good. More important, he doesn't just describe the emperor, he creates him. He doesn't just describe the city of Rome, or Athens, or whatever the subject of his panegyric might be: he creates the city as a socially valid and meaningful entity.

Surely this urge to create an emperor as a socially significant, comprehensible, and accessible reality is what lies behind the Roman custom of having the consul deliver a panegyric to the emperor on a regular basis. Without the panegyrist, the emperor is an alien in the empire he rules, an enigma as well as a disruption. The goal of the panegyrist is to make meaning out of the events, actions, and traits of character that led to the emperor's accession and that continue to shape his reign. Pliny as much as says this when he reminds his audience that the emperor Trajan, the matter of his panegyric, rejects private expressions of praise and thanksgiving, and accepts only the praise and thanksgiving that Pliny is right now, in his speech, actualizing. Precisely because panegyric invents the emperor it cannot be left to the unpredictable initiative of random individuals. What is more, Pliny openly admits that if the emperor who is the matter of the panegyric is bad, the panegyric, by, in effect, lying about him, puts him on notice as to how he is to behave (*Panegyricus* 4.2). In other words, the theatricality of panegyric, the self-conscious summoning up of an alternative reality, is precisely its point. Epideictic or panegyric, far from being a debased or decadent form of rhetoric, is of its essence.

The attempt on the part of the panegyrist to re-present his subject, to transform him from enigma to ideal, characterizes individual portions of Pliny's *Panegyricus* as well as the speech as a whole. Indeed, Pliny's *Panegyricus* is noteworthy for its strong appeal to the senses of sight and sound. Over and over again Pliny summons up memorable images of aspects of Trajan's career (a technique of rhetorical style called *enargeia*). When he speaks of the military triumph celebrated by Trajan, he says: "I seem to see [*cernere*] a triumph, one weighted down not with the spoils of provinces but with the weapons of enemies and the chains of conquered kings" (*Panegyricus* 17.2). When he praises Trajan for ridding the city of informants (*delatores*), he insists that his audience "keep in mind this image [Latin *facies*]: the fleet of the informants buffeted by every wind, the sails forced to endure the storms, to press on over angry seas, the informants themselves scrambling on the rocks" where their ships had foundered (*Panegyricus* 35.1). Even the buildings and monuments constructed by Trajan, which, presumably, members of the audience could go and look at for themselves, are enargistically summoned through Pliny's language. Indeed, Pliny emphasizes precisely the enigmatic way in which they came into being: for him, the porticoes and temples shot up so quickly it is as if they are just refurbished versions of buildings that were always already there. The magical power of the emperor to transform the urban landscape is matched by the magical power of the orator to constitute the social significance of monuments and, what is more, to retroject that significance into an authorizing past.

It will come as no surprise that the visions summoned by the *Panegyricus* are reinforced through application of all the stylistic effects years of rhetorical training inculcated in the master craftsman Pliny. Memorable *sententiae*, or concise sayings, are scattered throughout (albeit difficult to render into English): *ut pater patriae esses ante quam fieres* – "you already were father of the country before you were so named" (*Panegyricus* 21.1); *nec ducum quisquam aut non amari a militibus aut amari timet* – "no longer do generals have to fear either being loved by their soldiers, or not" (*Panegyricus* 18.2); *frustra se terrore succinxerit, qui saeptus caritate non fuerit* – "there's no point in attacking others with terror if you haven't defended yourself with generosity" (*Panegyricus* 49.3). Apostrophe is used to address the deceased emperor Nerva (*Panegyricus* 89.1). Personification enlivens the description of the serenity of the emperor's palace (*Panegyricus* 47.6). A metaphor drawn from the night sky illuminates the relationship between the emperor and other members of the Roman elite (*Panegyricus* 47.6). Aposiopesis (the breaking off of a thought in midstream) conveys the agitation of the speaker who presents himself as incapable of communicating the quantity of Trajan's achievements

(*Panegyricus* 28.1). Parallelism, isocolon, anaphora, alliteration run rampant: to take but one example, the sententia cited above on the relationship between terror and generosity contains two clauses of virtually identical length, the first and last word of the sententia start with the same letter (f), t's, s's, and c's unify the interior, and the conclusion of the two clauses constitutes a virtual rhyme. What is more, while every word in the sententia as quoted starts with a consonant, the phrase that follows in the original Latin contains nothing but words starting with vowels – *armis enim arma irritantur* ("aggression evidently activates aggression"). The inevitable outcome of Domitian's paranoid behavior is conveyed in a non-stop rush of language.

In the case of Aelius Aristides' panegyric of Rome we have the even more peculiar – to a modern audience – instance of an orator from afar eulogizing the city of Rome to the Romans themselves. At first, Aristides would seem to adopt a modern notion of the relationship between speech and subject, for he insists that no oration could possibly match the greatness of Rome. It quickly turns out, though, that this mismatch is due not to the inevitable limitations of speech but to the unprecedented grandeur of Rome. Indeed, it is precisely because there is no vantage point from which one can see all of Rome that Rome cannot be adequately represented in speech. This opening gambit, while it confirms our emphasis on the enargistic function of panegyric, would still seem to be something of a rhetorical dead-end or, at best, a trite appeal for the audience's sympathy (although surely they would have been more sympathetic if Aelius had simply never attempted an impossible topic). In reality, it prepares the way for what seems to be Aelius Aristides' real topic, announced in his play on the meaning of the Greek common noun *rome*: "strength" or "power." What Aelius proposes to represent to the Romans is an image not so much of the city they can see, if only partially, before them, but of their power: the strength of the Romans, their political, military, economic, and spiritual preeminence in relationship to past empires and current human communities.

In organizing his speech around comparison of Rome with past and present political entities, Aristides is following the advice of the handbooks dating back at least to the *Rhetoric for Alexander*, for they identify comparison with others in the same category as an important component of epideixis. In addition, as the handbooks routinely recommend, Aristides pays less attention to the accidental circumstances of Rome's success (e.g., location and climate) and more to the purposeful activities of the Romans. He even acknowledges the special characteristics of the audience (in this case the Romans themselves), as Aristotle advises and Quintilian confirms. Almost at the outset of the speech Aristides asks the Romans to aid his endeavor so that by contact with their cultivation he who was formerly uncultured may become "tuneful and clever."[3] The compliment may be an allusion to a previous trip to Rome during which Aristides, felled by a cold (or so he says: he is antiquity's most notorious hypochondriac), delivered a dreadful oration. But it also plays on traditional Roman anxieties about the alleged superiority of Greek culture. In effect, Aristides acknowledges the anxieties while at the same time suggesting, even demonstrating, that they are ungrounded. The better the ensuing speech, the greater and more immediate the evidence of Rome and the Romans' positive impact on everything and everyone they encounter.

Another piece of handbook advice helps bring to light the deeper aims of Aristides' speech and of panegyric in general. In summing up his chapter on the topics appropriate to speeches of praise and blame, Quintilian remarks: "really, all of praise resembles exercises in persuasion, since for the most part the same things that are praised in the one case are advised in the other" (*Institutio Oratoria* 3.7.28). In other words, laudation and exhortation differ in structure and context, but not in aim. To praise something or someone is to exhort it to behave in a certain way. So, too, the actions selected for praise are those that the speaker wishes the object of praise – provided it's sentient – to continue to carry out, or, if the actions praised stretch the truth, to undertake. Sentiments that strike the modern reader as indications of the speaker's obsequiousness can in fact be understood as implicit expressions of advice. Thus, when Aristides describes the Roman empire as a chorus and the emperor as chorus leader, he's not just amplifying Rome's glory or, for that matter, passing over the bleaker aspects of her relations with subject communities. Rather, he is struggling to present a model of interaction among the parts of the empire that moves beyond hierarchical structures of command: in choral song and dance, success depends on the cooperation of all sectors, and the leader is himself a part of the ultimate performance. So, too, Aristides' description of the Roman empire as a democracy, absurd on the face of it, in fact calls attention to aspects of Roman social structure he wants to see continue: for Aristides, democracy implies an equal right to participation, but only for the more powerful in the various communities. In effect, the elites throughout the empire, regardless of language or ethnicity, together form the equivalent of the demos in a Greek polis. Just as democracy reduced the importance of class distinctions within the citizen body, so too the Roman empire is praised for – and following Quintilian's logic, urged to continue – treating members of the leadership class, regardless of origin, as equals.

As we noted in an earlier chapter, the funeral orations delivered by Pericles and other carefully selected Athenians can be understood as "inventing" the city: giving it a sense of itself that, if not true, is nonetheless effective. Indeed, it was my contention that Thucydides cites the Funeral Oration of Pericles early in his history not just to call attention to the contrast between Periclean idealism and Athenian reality, but also to document how an idea of Athens sustained her citizens through years of exhausting war. Something comparable is going on with panegyric in the Roman empire. Pliny uses the occasion of the panegyric of Trajan to invent an ideal of the emperor that constrains the entire audience – not just the citizens and senators who might be expected to put aside reservations or objections and adhere to the myth of Trajan's incommensurability, but also Trajan himself, who is made to hear what it is the dominant sector of society admires, or hopes to admire, about his rule. In the case of Aristides' panegyric of Rome, the stakes are even higher, since Aristides hopes to impose upon his audience an image of the very essence of Rome – its *rome*. Once again, an enigma, a mystery beyond everyday perception, is materialized in language. And that materialization – or so the orator hopes – takes on a life of its own, thanks to the speed, character, clarity, awesomeness, etc., of his performance.

Much had changed in the ancient Mediterranean world between the time of Pericles (which was also the time of the sophists) and the time of Pliny and Trajan or of Aelius Aristides and his emperor Antoninus Pius. Certainly, the charisma of oratory now shone more brightly from epideixis and panegyric than from deliberation and courtroom success. But the basic function of rhetoric and oratory – to serve as the special speech of the state, the bulwark against the disordering powers of language (and much else) – persisted. In Aelius Aristides' own life experience, obsession with the healing of troubled bodies and spirits permeates both his devotion to the god Asclepius and his commitment to oratory as a sacred calling – indeed, he seems unable to resist listing the spread of the worship of Asclepius among the many fruits of the peace presided over by Rome. But what has happened between Pericles and Aristides, as the present chapter has attempted to make clear, is that the craft of rhetoric has emerged and proliferated as a means of transmitting and multiplying the power of the singer to gain access to the world beyond the here and now.

Aristides ends his praise of Rome by likening its success to the triumph of the Olympian gods over uproar and disorder. He says that Homer foresaw the Romans' empire, and that Hesiod would have – if only he had been "a more perfect poet" and "endowed with the same power of divination" as Homer enjoyed ("Regarding Rome" 106).[4] By situating Rome within a tradition commencing with Homer and Hesiod, Aristides of course invites continuing respect for the Greek culture he represents on the part of his Roman audience. There is a hint as well that he, as orator, now occupies the social position of the archaic poet-prophet. If so, however, it is a position he has earned by continually struggling to become "more perfect" as a speaker, that is to say, by mastering the craft of rhetoric.

4

Rhetoric as Acculturation

Rhetoric was the pinnacle of ancient education. While some students undertook advanced studies in philosophy or mathematics alongside of or in place of rhetoric, the majority of ambitious students completed their formal education with training in rhetoric. Rhetorical study was in effect the last of a three-stage educational process, one that led the student from elementary study of reading, writing, and arithmetic, through intensive work in literary interpretation at the school of the grammaticus, and on to training with teachers of rhetoric known variously as rhetores and sophistai. Each stage of education was progressively more exclusive, with students winnowed on the basis of talent, family resources, and gender: girls, no matter how gifted or well-off, never proceeded to the school of the rhetorician. In addition, each stage took the student literally and figuratively farther from home. Elementary education was available even in rural villages, literary training less so, and rhetoric not at all. For most students, attendance at rhetoric school entailed an extended stay in one of a handful of great urban centers, such as Rome, Athens, Alexandria, Antioch, or Pergamum.

Rhetoric built on the earlier stages of education, which in certain respects were geared toward it. Thus the student of rhetoric might well return to some of the same literary texts (e.g., Homer's *Iliad*, Vergil's *Aeneid*) through which he had first learned to read, only now with an eye toward imitation of stylistic effects or isolation of strategies of character construction. Composition of the narrative portion of a speech presupposed mastery of preliminary, or progymnastic, exercises in storytelling. Memorization of detailed arguments or long verbatim speeches – the type of feat that still strikes modern readers as improbable – was possible because the student had been cultivating his memory from the beginning of elementary school, where he learned to recite and write the alphabet forwards and backwards, to generate complex matrices of all possible syllables, and to recite long passages of poetry by heart. Rhetorical training intensified the respect for tradition, role playing, verbal alacrity, and mental gymnastics that characterized ancient education more generally. But it also effected its own distinctive transformation of the student, differentiating him in both degree and kind from those who had not studied rhetoric. Because this transformation often entailed a permanent migration from one culture to another (e.g., Egyptian to Greek, Spanish or Gallic to Roman), and because it encompassed attitudes, practices, and beliefs, indeed the student's very sense of self, it is helpful to regard rhetorical training not just as acquisition of knowledge, but more generally as a process of acculturation. Indeed, we might go so far as to say that rhetoric becomes its own culture into which the student is gradually initiated.

The components of rhetorical culture – as of any culture – are mixed and can be understood both as characteristic practices of a group and as attainments of an individual. Key ancient texts that argue for the indispensability of rhetorical training waver on precisely this point: are they articulating a set of cultural ideals or proposing an individual role model as a pattern for imitation? For example, the final book of Quintilian's *Institutio Oratoria* argues that the end of rhetoric is the formation of a *Romanus sapiens*: someone who combines the wisdom of a Greek sage with the practicality of a Roman man of action. Quintilian expresses doubt that anyone has ever achieved the ideal, yet he continually refers his reader to the biography of Cicero for evidence of what the ideal, if realized, would look like. He advances a cultural ideal that he hopes will transform the outlook and practice of each student. In his mingling of goals for cultural and personal transformation, as well as in the specific nature of those goals, he echoes the writings of Isocrates and Cicero before him, and furthermore provides a framework for understanding the scraps of evidence from the rhetorical schools themselves – evidence that survives in the form of inscriptions, papyri, drawings, sculpture, reliefs, and archeological remains, as well as literary and biographical anecdotes from throughout the Greco-Roman world. What this large body of material, viewed comprehensively, suggests is that the personal and cultural transformations brought about by rhetoric involve language, relationship to tradition, gender identity, modes of interpersonal interaction, patterns of thought, and political affiliations. In short, becoming rhetorical, or becoming eloquent, as the ancients would say, by reshaping individual subjectivity, reshapes culture – and vice versa.

Let us begin with language. Despite our tendency to speak of "Greco-Roman" civilization, in fact the ancient Mediterranean world encompassed speakers of dozens of languages and dialects. From an early stage, shared language became one of the features through which inhabitants of Greek city-states defined themselves as Greek. This shared sense of Greekness, based upon linguistic and to a lesser extent cultural unity, served the Greeks well in their struggles with neighboring peoples, from the Persian empire in the East to the indigenous populations dominated by Greek colonizers in the islands and coastal regions of the Mediterranean and Black Seas. In time, Alexander the Great, his soldiers, and the merchants and craftsmen who followed in their wake, brought or reinforced the use of Greek throughout the lands of the Eastern Mediterranean and Western Asia, including Mesopotamia, ancient Persia, and some or all of modern-day Afghanistan, Ukraine, Pakistan, and India. While modern scholars debate the extent to which Greek language and Greek cultural patterns permeated the life of the regions conquered by Alexander, it is clear that at least among the elite sectors of the population the Greek language provided a useful means of communication over geographical and cultural boundaries. It also served to differentiate mobile, educated sectors of the population from those who spent most, if not all, of their lives in the vicinity of their native villages.

A similar pattern obtained with the spread of Latin. Initially just the language of the seven hills of Rome and its agricultural hinterland, Latin became a marker of Romanness precisely as the Romans entered into competition and conflict with other powerful peoples, such as Samnites, Carthaginians, Celts, and Macedonians. There is little evidence that the Romans imposed Latin on the populations they conquered; rather, the need for subordinate peoples to communicate with their overlords, as well as the prestige associated with Latin, prompted its spread throughout the Western Mediterranean. The fact that Latin penetrated more deeply into lands such as Gaul, Spain, and Dacia (modern Romania) than into Greek-speaking areas that were also subject to Roman control is worth reflecting on. It suggests that it was not linguistic chauvinism per se that led to the spread of Latin so much as the usefulness of a lingua franca in promoting political and economic integration. Where that lingua franca already existed (i.e., in Greek-speaking portions of the empire), the Romans saw no need to replace it. In effect, their empire was, from an administrative standpoint, bilingual. Moreover, in many parts of the West, the absence of city-state organization prior to the coming of the Romans (or their destruction of such organization in the course of conquest) meant that they brought with them institutions such as schools, lawcourts, treaties, and the like, which in the Greek-speaking East already existed, and thus did not have to be created. Finally, as recent archeological and epigraphical discoveries make clear, the city of Rome itself was always already multilingual and multicultural, with Greek merchants and craftsmen in particular instrumental in its growth from an early stage. As a result, Romans showed greater comprehension of and respect for Hellenic institutions in territories they acquired than for the institutions and cultural practices of non-Greek peoples.

Rhetoric, as the culmination of a system of education based on cultivation of the Greek and/or Latin languages, intensified their linguistic hegemony. Especially in the period of the Roman empire, rhetorical education secured the identification of the elite sectors of the population with a larger community of Greek and Latin speakers. Rhetoric did not exactly wipe out indigenous languages, traces of which survived throughout the Mediterranean long after the arrival of Greeks and Romans: Getic alongside Greek in Tomis, so-called demotic alongside Greek in Egypt, Oscan alongside Latin in Pompeii, to name just a few examples. However, rhetoric did redirect the creative energies of the educated sector of the population toward the production of texts in Latin and Greek, with the result that the linguistic diversity of the classical world is not matched by an equivalent diversification of surviving literature from that world. Indeed, a strikingly high proportion of surviving texts of so-called Greek and Latin authors were not composed by native speakers of Greek or Latin, certainly not of the dialects of Greek and Latin that are best represented among the texts.

The language of classical rhetoric, despite its use in everyday circumstances of political, legal, and academic discourse, bears some of the marks of what is known as a *Kunstsprache*, or artificial type of speech. It had to be learned, in school, by everyone who used it – the way, at a later period, ecclesiastical Latin had to be learned as a new language, or at least a new dialect, by almost everyone who used it.

The foreignness of the language of rhetoric might well be viewed as one of its strengths. Native to no one, it could be mastered, in theory, by anyone with time and money to pursue it. Moreover, mastery of rhetorical language, especially since it entailed removal of the student from the home environment at precisely the age of transition from childhood to adulthood, contributed to a sense of shared community among its users, regardless of origin. The usefulness of a lingua franca (or, to cite the Greek term, *koinê*), together with the expenditure of time and effort required to acquire it, created a perpetually reinforcing feedback mechanism that gave rhetoric something of a life of its own: a development we have already alluded to in our discussion of the seemingly inexplicable proliferation of rhetorical handbooks constantly dwelling on the same – or almost the same – esoteric points of doctrine.

The self-sustaining aspect of rhetoric also led to its stabilization over time. Everyday language changes as a matter of course. Language that is reinforced by an educational system, especially one built on the analysis, performance, and imitation of canonical texts, changes more slowly. Again, this phenomenon is hardly unique to ancient Greece and Rome: ecclesiastical Latin and academic French are two well-known parallels. But because rhetoric, in addition to being an identifying badge of membership in a trans-historical elite, was also a practice vital to the administration of cities, lawcourts, and empires, its language (or languages, Greek and Latin) were subject to competing pressures toward stability and adaptation. Some of the fiercest intra-rhetorical battles were waged over precisely the question of how much change to allow in the language of the schools and the forum. The first salvo may have been fired by Alexandrian scholars, who privileged canonical representatives of various literary genres – although the standard list of ten Attic orators seems not to have stabilized until the Roman period. In time, even Cicero was subject to attack for not being "Attic" enough, that is, for incorporating stylistic elements that allegedly corrupted the purity of Roman speech in the same way that contemporary speakers of Greek in Asia Minor were alleged to have corrupted the purity of classical Athenian speech. Cicero retaliated by arguing for a more flexible and inclusive approach to language and style, only to be turned, after his death and canonization in the schools, into a stick with which to beat later generations of adapters. Eventually, though, he again came to seem not quite classical enough for the purists, and during the Hadrianic period there is even something of a revival of interest in the prickly style of archaic, or pre-Ciceronian, Latin prose.

It is easy to see the ongoing struggle over stabilizing versus expansive approaches to language as mirroring political conflicts over inclusive versus exclusive approaches to governance and recruitment to the elites. Oddly enough, this struggle also seems to reflect – and generate: there's the feedback mechanism again – a perpetual crisis over the nature of elite masculinity. A speaker cannot function politically and socially simply by replicating the language of his predecessors, but how far can he venture from that language without betraying the group with which he has chosen to identify through his rhetorical education? So, too, he cannot be a man in exactly the way his ancestors were men – in particular, the very power of rhetoric, as we saw in the opening chapter, derives from its association with the arts of peace as opposed to the arts of war. But how far can he venture from inherited protocols of masculinity without being something other than a man? Here, modern notions of gender as a performance, rather than an innate set of dispositions or characteristics, are anticipated by ancient rhetoric's obsessive concern with issues of gender identity, especially with respect to rhetorical performance – what the Greeks called *hypokrisis* and the Romans classified as *actio*.

Rhetoric's concern with manliness is omnipresent. Greek orators accuse one another of failure to live up to culturally specific standards of masculinity from at least the time of Demosthenes onward. Gorgias and Isocrates must defend themselves, implicitly or explicitly, against the accusation that to immerse oneself in the pleasures of rhetoric is to succumb to the charms of the goddess Persuasion, or Peitho. At Rome, the earliest definition of the orator emphasizes his status as an elite male. According to Cato the Elder, the orator is a *vir bonus, dicendi peritus*. The phrase loosely translates as "a good man, skilled at speaking," but each term in it is laden with social significance. In particular, *vir* implies not just biological maleness, but the distinctive masculinity of the free, autonomous citizen, while the supplementary adjective *bonus* emphasizes that he behaves in accordance with traditional codes of conduct.

As the production of rhetorical treatises proliferates, anxiety over the reproduction of legitimate male subjects intensifies. Terms for style are often virtual codewords for gender identity or sexual role: soft, hard, manly, languid, forceful, submissive, fiery, frigid. Bodily deportment and voice are subject to particular scrutiny both by instructors of rhetoric and by peers involved in the give and take of verbal combat in school, courtroom, or assembly. According to Quintilian, the orator must avoid unmanly movements, especially the sort that make one appear to be dancing (*Institutes* 11.3.128). His grooming and dress should be attractive but manly (*Institutes* 11.3.137) – there's a proper hemline for men, another for women (*Institutes* 11.3.138–9). The toga, that mark of elite male status and sexual autonomy, takes on a gender identity all by itself: if managed properly it "assumes a combative pose" (*Institutes* 11.3.145), if badly, it becomes if not quite "insane" (*furiosus*, at *Institutes* 11.3.146) then surely "licentious and fey" (*solutus ac delicatus*, at *Institutes* 11.3.146). Quintilian's insistence on the gendered nature of performance is matched by the imperial Greek writers' attention to voice. Over and over again the orators of the second sophistic rely on vocal as well as visual cues to identify their rivals as *cinaedi*: in effect, sexually suggestive male dancers, or men who behave like sexually suggestive dancers in their encounters with other men.

Yet the use of rhetorical terminology and guidelines to construct and enforce boundaries between acceptable and unacceptable masculine behavior has a curious double edge to it. Even as the rhetoricians insist on the need not to cross the boundary between proper and improper male behavior, they continually reveal that just such a boundary can be crossed, and in either direction. The more they work to train students in ideal masculine performance, the more they expose the very performative nature of ideal masculinity. For example, in an anecdote concerning Cicero's rival Hortensius, we are told that Hortensius' gestures while speaking were so expressive that another orator took to calling him Dionysia, after a renowned female dancer of mimes (Aulus Gellius, *Attic Nights* 1.5.3). That the charge was one of gender irregularity and not mastery of the wrong craft is clear from Hortensius' reported response, since "he answered in a mincing but good-humored way: 'I'd much rather be Dionysia than what you are, Torquatus – uncultivated, undersexed, and as undionysian as they come!'" By showing that effeminacy is a role he can adopt or reject at a moment's notice, Hortensius asserts his essential masculinity, while at the same time suggesting that Torquatus' notion of what it is to be a man is really just unappealing boorishness, a retreat, in effect, to a pre-rhetorical state of being. As for the properly masculine voice, Quintilian precedes his long and extremely informative chapter on voice by expressly denying the claim that delivery, of which voice is a key component, can be attained solely by obeying natural impulse (*Institutes* 11.3.11). In fact, an elaborate procedure of vocal training is recommended, although it is to be applied only sparingly during adolescence, when all the organs "start to grow and thus are tender and susceptible to injury" (*Institutes* 11.3.29).

A number of possible reasons have been offered for this close association between rhetorical culture and masculinity. Some scholars, paying special attention to the material from the Roman empire, suggest that the superimposition of an all-powerful emperor on a system of elite male competition creates an ongoing crisis of masculinity, a situation in which all men must admit that they are in some sense subordinate to another man. While there is no doubt some truth to such an account, especially when applied to the men who were, absent the emperor, at the top of the social hierarchy, it cannot be the whole story, since the policing of male behavior is a characteristic of rhetoric and oratory long before the coming of the Roman principate and extends farther down the ladder of social hierarchy than the top rungs to which the emperor might be expected to pay close attention. Others see in rhetoric a rejection of any and all stable categories of being: awareness of and anxiety over masculinity as a construct is thus just one manifestation of a more widespread concern with the instability of meaning. The recurrence of such a concern is a kind of "return of the repressed," since the instability of language and meaning runs afoul of rhetoric's role in the replication of a social elite from one generation to the next. Seneca the Elder seems to have a diagnosis of this sort in mind when he introduces his treatise on declamations by denouncing contemporaries who misuse great rhetoric of the past by taking it out of context. As he puts it, "the sacred rite of eloquence, which they cannot perform, they never fail to deform" (Seneca, *Controversies* 1 pref. 10).

A third approach might supplement the first two by focusing more narrowly on rhetoric's role in social replication, or as we have been discussing in this chapter, acculturation. Training in rhetoric requires the youthful male to experience separation from the female: as noted earlier, girls could join in elementary and literary education, but not in rhetorical education; and boys who proceeded to rhetoric school by and large did so by leaving home. Thus we might expect the boundaries between maleness and femaleness to be of particular concern in the rhetorical context. Moreover, rhetoric, precisely because it invites transition to a new or at least more expansive culture than that of the native household and community, creates a relationship of desire or aspiration between the young male and adult males other than his father: teachers, older students, celebrity orators, patrons and the like. Indeed, at least during the Roman republic, this psychological aspect of acculturation was realized in the institution of *tirocinium fori*, whereby a young man, upon completing his formal education, was "handed over" – the verb used (*deduco*) being the same as that of the "handing over" of a bride – not to a husband, but to a responsible older male in the community who would complete the youth's entree into society. In other words, rhetoric can hardly avoid being about the precariousness of masculinity since one of its key social functions is to serve as gatekeeper to elite male status.

If we situate the individual student into this broader social framework of acculturation, we begin to get a sense of how education more generally and rhetorical training in particular shape his developing sense of self. His early school exercises, as one scholar has noted, train him in the use of the imperative and encourage him to think of himself, the *vir*-in-training, as the center of attention for all in the household. Literary study, which culminates in the dramatic recitation of favored texts, teaches him to impersonate a wide variety of characters, from slaves to gods, foreigners to Roman heroes, male and female, young and old, indiscriminately. Then, as part of his formal rhetorical training – and also as a form of entertainment during adulthood – he declaims, sometimes on general theses (e.g., should a man marry?), sometimes on pivotal historical moments (should Xerxes cross the Hellespont? should Cicero beg for his life?), eventually on made-up legal cases that challenge him to consider conflicts between seemingly reasonable laws or unpredictable collisions of law and circumstance. Although fantastic, the topics of these fictional cases, or *controversiae*, many of which are preserved by Seneca the Elder, are hardly random. Over and over again the controversiae require the student to consider relations between fathers and sons, men and women, and powerful men and their social inferiors.

As an example of a topic for declamation we may consider the case of the pirate chief's daughter (Seneca the Elder, *Controversies* 1.6). According to the premise of the exercise, a son who was captured by pirates unsuccessfully appealed to his father for ransom. Thereupon the daughter of the pirate chief arranged the release of the son on condition that he marry her. Having done so and returned home, the son was ordered by his father to divorce his pirate princess of a wife and marry an orphan (i.e., a woman whose property is up for grabs). The topic gives plenty of opportunity for discussion of social status and wealth, for speculation on the true background of the pirate's daughter or on the likelihood that such a marriage could produce noble offspring. The declaimer can expatiate on the relationship between birth and character or on the dangers of a rich wife (presuming it is to gain control of her wealth that the father wants the son to marry the orphan). Elaborate contrasts are developed between enslavement in a pirate camp and enslavement to a wife. What is not really spoken of, and yet must lie at the heart of the declamation, is the younger male's need to negotiate a certain degree of autonomy with respect to his father without resorting to flat-out disobedience or rebellion. In a sense, the declamation permits him to fantasize about running off with the girl of his dreams in violation of his father's wishes.

Fantasy of another sort may figure in the theme of the double rapist. According to this controversia (Seneca the Elder, *Controversies* 1.5), the law provides that a rape victim gets to choose between having the rapist executed or making him marry her. What happens if a man rapes two women in one night, with one demanding execution and the other insisting on marriage? In one sense, the topic invites a certain trivialization of the crime of rape: some declaimers imagine that the one woman was not really raped, just angling to get a husband; others suggest that the victim who insists on execution is jealous of her rival; yet another declaimer wonders what would have happened if both women had chosen marriage – would they go to court over a man who had violated them? The theme also allows for a great deal of ranting and raving about the contemporary state of morals and provides an opportunity to adopt a suitably punitive tone, with several declaimers suggesting that it is fine for the rapist to marry as long as he is subsequently executed and others arguing (sensibly enough) that a decision in favor of marriage would provide an incentive for rapists to repeat their crime in order to increase the odds that one victim would select marriage. Again, as with the theme of the pirate's daughter, the topic of controversy raises, only to avoid, difficult questions concerning the male–female relations at the heart of the social structure: when is a woman ever allowed to choose her husband? Under what circumstances can she say no? Indeed, the word for rape used in the topic is *rapio*, which also means "steal," in opposition to the more obvious term for sexual debasement, namely *stuprum*. The whole set-up alludes to the fact that from a certain standpoint all women are just property to be "taken" or "stolen" from one household to another, that what we call rape is construed by ancient men as theft from the father of the daughter's chastity, which, if left intact, he can use to establish a relationship of exchange with another male. What is more, the fact that the victim can marry her assailant without a dowry (this is specified in the premise of the case) exposes the economic basis of marriage by suggesting that a husband – if obtained for free – might well be a fair exchange for undergoing rape. The snippets of declamation preserved by Seneca come close to articulating the gender inequality at the heart of the institution of marriage, only to shy away from it: as Seneca reports, one declaimer – much to Seneca's consternation – was praised for his terse suggestion that the rapist in question "should stick to men" (*Controversies* 1.5.9).

Relations between fathers and sons and between men and women preoccupy the declaimers. So too, unsurprisingly, does the figure of the tyrant. As indicated in an earlier chapter, the tyrant is a looming presence throughout the rhetorical tradition because he and he alone creates the political conditions of statehood whereby rhetoric can come into existence. But in the declamatory tradition the tyrant does additional work, since he reminds the declaimer and his audience of the reality of servitude. A declamation about a tyrant is in effect a declamation about the problem of mastery. Thus, another controversia (Seneca the Elder, *Controversies* 7.6) posits a situation in which a tyrant grants to slaves permission to kill their masters and rape their mistresses. According to the premise, the leading men of the state flee abroad and all the slaves take advantage of the situation with the exception of one, who preserves the virginity of his freeborn mistress. When her father returns from exile he gives her to the slave in marriage, whereupon his son (the young woman's brother) brings a charge of insanity against the father. The case invites consideration of the possibility of reversal of fortune, of the permeability of the boundary between slave and free – only to set up elaborate defenses against it. Little is said in support of the father, nothing from the vantage point of the slave. Instead, the speakers compete to find cleverer ways to bemoan the sufferings of the sister and the madness of the father. One glances in the direction of the slave, only to argue that now he is being deprived of a slave's greatest honor, the chance to preserve the virginity of his mistress. Another defends the father on the basis of precedent, noting that even Cato married the daughter of a freedwoman. But others will have nothing to do with this argument, hammering away at the difference between freed and freeborn, and between Cato and the father in this case. In short, a topic that might have explored the common humanity of slave and free bogs down in discussion of the mental and ethical status of freeborn males, present and past.

In considering, if only to reject, the possibility of sons who rebel against their fathers, women who make unconstrained choices about their life situations, and slaves who are morally equivalent to free men, declamation plays at the boundaries of the culture into which the student of rhetoric is acculturated. This boundary work reminds the modern reader of the less appealing aspects of ancient civilizations, even as it suggests that those aspects were never entirely repressed by the ancients themselves. When we move to the heart of rhetorical culture, we encounter practices and beliefs that are less disturbing to the modern reader, in some respects even inspiring.

Perhaps most obvious is the way in which rhetoric encouraged an astonishing mental alacrity. Alertness and versatility are much admired by Seneca and his declaimers, and appear as the stock-in-trade of Greek declaimers as well. The content of the declamation concerning the man who raped two women in one night may be repugnant, but the form of the problem – how to reconcile the obvious intent of the law with unexpected circumstances – forces the declaimer to reflect on issues crucial to the maintenance of a legitimate judicial system over time. Similarly, a wildly improbable situation requires the rhetor and his audience to consider the tension between "literalist" and "activist" interpretations of the law: for example, one Greek rhetorical thesis asks whether a sophist is responsible for the actions of those who commit suicide after hearing his paradoxical encomium on death; a common thesis asks whether someone whose weeping causes fellow citizens to rebel is guilty of treason. And topics that hinge on the apparent verbal ambiguity of laws, wills, treaties, and so on, would not (with appropriate changes) be out of place in a courtroom today: did the deceased leave his estate "entirely to Leon" or "to Pantaleon?" (*panta leonti* or *pantaleonti?*: Sopatros, *Rhetores Graeci* 8.377). Such concerns find expression at Greece and Rome in other contexts as well, such as tragedy and epic, which ponder the clash of competing goods, or recurrent stories about the ambiguous meaning of oracles and the dire consequences that befall those who interpret them wrongly. In declamation, as in rhetorical practice more generally, we find such considerations transferred from the religious to the secular realm and subject to rule-bound scrutiny: in effect, they become problems to be resolved by the state and its institutions rather than mysterious dangers to be contained by ritual and myth.

Along with mental alacrity, then, comes a deep respect for rules. While those who share collectively in rhetorical culture may be unwilling to yield the social and political advantages they have over the rest of society, within the realm of rhetoric all agree to abide by the judgment of others. Such judgment may not always be logical or fair, but it is reached by rules that are agreed on in advance. Indeed, one of the remarkable features of the surviving declamations is the lack of argument over the admissibility or inadmissibility of opposing arguments. Even in orations composed for real, as opposed to fictional cases, while the testimony of witnesses may be impugned, minimized, or contradicted, orators rarely if ever ask that it be excluded. Such a failure may to some extent be an accident of transmission; but even that would be telling, since it would suggest that no one wanted to go on record as having won a case by crying foul.

Instead of learning to argue about procedures, students of rhetoric trained themselves to present what was given in the best possible light. This is the point of learning to argue both sides of the same question – not to become ethically obtuse, as critics of rhetoric both ancient and modern sometimes imply – but to make the most of whatever comes one's way. Once in a while Seneca the Elder speaks of students being unwilling to take one side or the other of a case. But in the overwhelming majority of controversiae and suasoriae he can find someone to develop an interesting *color* or compose an incisive sententia in favor of the most preposterous position. In modern America a defense attorney will sometimes be heard to explain his or her defense of a client he believes to be guilty on the grounds that "the system" requires that everyone be given the best possible defense or that a good defense forces the prosecution to behave responsibly. This is not quite the position of the ancient rhetorician, however. His interest in probing both sides of an issue derives from a belief, not that the truth exists independent of discourse and is to be found through inquiry, but that the truth of a case is socially determined by the give and take of opposing, even multiple, perspectives. For all that ancient rhetoric is socially elitist, it is epistemologically democratic.

This tendency to consider all participants in oratory and rhetoric as contributing to the truth goes back at least as far as the sophists.

It was they after all who insisted that the art of speaking could be taught, in other words that it was not the unique possession of the naturally gifted. From Protagoras' definition of "man as the measure of all things" to the various sophistic reflections on the origin of justice in human interaction, the sophists seek both to deprive human institutions of any transcendent authorization and to make possible the construction of a just society through logos, that is, reasoned speech. The characteristic sophistic rhetorical structure of antilogy – argument on both sides of the same issue – rather than inducing a paralyzing skepticism, invites participation and judgment by members of the audience. In contrast, Plato's dialogues, for all that they involve question and answer and present multiple perspectives, aim to reorient the reader's perceptions, beliefs, and practices in a particular direction.

It is precisely this Platonic dialogue form, and its lost successors in Hellenistic philosophy, that Cicero repeatedly rejects in structuring his influential philosophical and rhetorical treatises. Like the sophists, he prefers to lay out competing sides of an issue, even such a seemingly fundamental issue as the "nature of the gods" or the proper form of the republic. In particular, his *De Oratore*, which is perhaps the preeminent defense of rhetorical culture that survives for us from antiquity, gives more or less equal time to the two main interlocutors, the older Roman orators and statesmen Antonius and Crassus. Antonius and Crassus take different sides on the question of the relative importance of nature and nurture in the formation of the orator, yet their disagreement, far from leading to victory for one point of view or confusion for the reader, ends up enriching the account of oratory for all involved. The very form of the Ciceronian dialogue, with its lengthy speeches and genial conversation, rather than the intense dialectical inquiry that characterizes Plato's dialogues, enacts its commitment to the construction of truth as a social enterprise. Cicero is often described as an adherent to the philosophical school known as the New Academy, which preached a certain skepticism in matters of epistemology and ethics. But it is surely Cicero as heir and champion of the Roman rhetorical tradition who gravitates towards the teachings of the New Academy, rather than the other way around. In any event, if Cicero's stylistic inclusiveness was not always imitated by his successors, his commitment to shared inquiry and testing of ideas has never been rejected by the rhetorical tradition, ancient or modern. Cicero's denial of transcendence, much like that of the sophists, was positivist rather than deconstructive in ultimate impact. Indeed, one of Cicero's favorite targets is the Greek quibbler, or practitioner of *disputatio*, whose skill in demolition of arguments stands in opposition to the positive precepts and models for action constructed by himself and his fellow Romans. Cicero's identification of the Roman as a positive social thinker reappears throughout the ages, in a wide variety of Roman texts, and almost succeeds in eclipsing the contributions of his sophistic predecessors.

If rhetorical culture thus encourages a collective, albeit competitive, negotiation of truth, it nonetheless places a high premium on respect for tradition. To the modern reader, these two tendencies may seem conflicting: one progressivist, in certain respects anticipating the later European Enlightenment, the other conservative, even authoritarian. To identify rhetoric's rationality and its traditionalism as mutually exclusive is to misconstrue both, but especially its relationship to tradition. When a Greek or Roman who has been schooled in rhetoric (and thus in the classics of literature, study of which precedes rhetorical education) looks to tradition, he seeks not fixed guidelines or restrictive models but a body of raw material out of which he, in collaboration and competition with his contemporaries, fashions something new. That all the rhetors, declaimers, and orators are working with the same body of raw material, the same tradition, provides a coherence to their shared enterprise and a mutual comprehensibility to their inventions. Appeal to tradition does for them what ritualization of language and action did for their predecessors: it imposes order on the chaos of "the linguistically liberated imagination."[1] Classic works of literature, traditional declamatory themes, and classic models of oratorical style provide fixed points of reference for both form and content of new rhetorical productions. Quintilian says as much when he canonizes a fixed reading list of Greek and Roman authors for use in the training of orators. His ambitious set of recommendations is actually not so far removed from the curricula that can be reconstructed from other evidence, such as the treatises of the grammarians, the tradition of *scholia*, or commentaries on literary texts, and scraps of papyri that survive from use in schools. Moreover, the effect of an education based on the absorption of classical models is evident in the literary, oratorical, or declamatory performances of later authors, both Greek and Roman. Indeed, a recent study has shown that Greek declamations of the fourth through sixth centuries AD still give evidence of precise and detailed knowledge of oratorical classics of the fourth century BC.

Interestingly enough, the tradition that sustains both Greek and Roman oratory is not very expandable. That is to say, the initiate into rhetorical culture is not equally interested in displaying familiarity with the writings of all generations prior to his. Among the Greek declaimers of the later Roman empire, there is little allusion to oratory, indeed to any literature, later than Alexander the Great, who died in 323 BC. Similarly, Roman rhetoricians are little interested in figures beyond the age of Cicero. Modern scholars sometimes attribute this development to an alleged decline in quality of oratorical production after the commencement of the principate (a decline expressly repudi- ated by at least one of the interlocutors in Tacitus' *Dialogus*, as we saw in chapter 1). But it corresponds to another even more pronounced pattern not always correlated with it: namely, the tendency for Roman moralists not to cite ethical exempla post-dating the end of the republic, either. Indeed, it is as if all possibility of ethical goodness collapsed on the point of Cato the Younger's sword in 46 BC.

What the Greek and the Roman practices thus have in common is an implicit association of the raw material of rhetoric with the life of the polis or city-state. Once the Greek city-states are pushed off center stage by the Macedonian army, once the real communities of Athens, Sparta, and so on, are eclipsed by the imagined community of Hellenism, rhetoric ceases to replenish its stock of situations, prob- lems, and models. This is not to say that it becomes moribund. Quite the contrary, as we have seen, treatises swell in numbers and oratory continues to be of crucial social and political importance. (One need only read the first century AD writer Plutarch's treatise entitled *Precepts of Statecraft* to get a sense of how important rhetorical skill continues to be in the day-to-day operation of the cities scattered throughout the Roman empire.) Similarly, at Rome, the rise of Caesar and the establishment of the Augustan principate mark the final stage of the city-state's submersion in the empire. Indeed, a standard way of describing the development of the principate is to say that Roman political institutions finally caught up with the fact that Rome had been an empire for some time. Power shifted from an aristocratic senate and popular assemblies to a bureaucracy centered at Rome and a flexible military and administrative apparatus that aimed to integrate farflung provinces into a shared fatherland or, at the least, a stubbornly effective cultural hegemony. As with the spread of Hellenism in the wake of Alexander, the creation of a new, pan-Mediterranean Roman nation led to a shift in emphasis, but not a diminution, of the rhetorical enterprise. Indeed, we might say that in both the Greek-speaking and the Roman-speaking world, rhetoric kept the dream of the city-state alive in the context of empire. In general, the ancient approach to any tradition consisted not of sterile imitation but of the reanimation of prototypes. We might recall the death masks of predecessors worn at the Roman funeral: these *imagines*, as they were known, are activated in performance, their social authority revived anew on various ritual occasions. The Greek and Roman rhetoricians' reworking of the themes and situations of earlier oratory are, in like manner, a reanimation of ancestral prototypes. Only in the case of rhetoric, the prototypes being reanimated are not just the individual orators but also the collective enterprise of oratory as constitutive of the life of the state.

In the late Greek tradition of declamation, as analyzed by the scholar D. A. Russell, this sense of continually reviving the life of the classical city-state is especially clear. As Russell notes, for all the wildly varying topics and approaches represented in the declamations of figures like Sopatros, Libanius, and Choricius, certain features of what he calls "Sophistopolis" are constant. The state as imagined by the late declaimers is, if not always democratic in institutions, certainly democratic in spirit. Freedom of speech is taken for granted, as is class struggle between the rich and the poor, with the poor almost always having the moral upper hand. Heroes emerge, but only in defensive combat, since the reanimated city-state does not fight wars of aggression. As heroes, though, they run the risk of becoming tyrants, and so many declamatory themes and speeches grapple with the relationship between heroes and tyrants or with accusations against heroes who may or may not be acting like tyrants. All such imaginary cases and situations may seem far removed from the everyday life of Antioch or Gaza in the late Roman and early Byzantine empire. Indeed, declamation's preference for the poor seems to run directly contrary to the material wealth it brought its most successful practitioners. But by keeping alive an image of the city-state as locus of power, declamation provides ideological cover for less sensational uses of rhetoric in everyday contexts. It can't keep power from being redistributed in the direction of regional or empire-wide elites. However, it can keep that redistribution from disrupting the relative harmony of the local community. The ancient Greeks and Romans in effect found a way of enjoying the benefits of cultural globalism while maintaining the possibility and the autonomy of shared enterprise at the local level.

In the case of Roman declamation and later Roman rhetoric, the process of reanimation of prototypes is easily confused with nostalgia for the republic – by modern scholars, but also, at times, by the participants themselves. We might ask whether the epic poet Lucan, himself a product of the schools of declamation, seeks to awaken the ghost of the republic as a political system, or, more likely, to revive models of interpersonal interaction that are characteristic of the city-state but hard to sustain under an empire. From this perspective, the rhetorical energy that characterizes almost all post-Augustan Latin poetry, from Ovid through Lucan, Seneca, the Flavian epicists, and onward, is a constructive force, one that keeps alive the image of Rome as a polis and thus sustains the continuing use of rhetorical modes of interaction at a time when the historical conditions that brought them into being no longer obtain. Rhetoric continually reanimates the democratic spirit in an undemocratic environment of imperialism and cultural hegemony. It grants its most skilled practitioners access to political and social power while allowing them to imagine a world in which power is more equitably distributed.

Any practice that does ideological work of the sort I have ascribed here to rhetoric can be expected to show traces of its own contradictions. The tensions within rhetorical culture, between hierarchy and egalitarianism, elitism and democracy, city-state and empire, are made manifest in some of the most striking of the declamatory themes. In both Greek and Roman declamation, for all of their imitation of and respect for canonical predecessors, there are clear strains of aggression toward the founders of the rhetorical tradition. On the Greek side we have numerous declamatory themes concerning possible ways in which Demosthenes may have met his fate. Should he be made a public slave? Should he be allowed to end his own life for giving bad advice? Should he be handed over to Philip of Macedon? The Roman declaimers, too, were fixated on the fate of their founding father, Cicero. They imagined that he was murdered by a man whom he had previously defended successfully on a charge of parricide. They pondered whether he should beg Antony's forgiveness for writing and delivering the Philippics. They imagined themselves advising him on the question should he die or burn his books.

In these declamatory themes the personal and the social aspects of rhetorical culture and rhetoric as acculturation are again intertwined. The declaimer is invited, in a sense, to kill the father(s) of rhetoric in order to assume his role as an adult in the rhetorical community, as well as in the community at large. In the Roman case, the psychological complexity of this invitation is especially acute, since so many of the new rhetoricians are men whose families are in the ascendant precisely because of the destruction of the republican aristocracy. Indeed, the whole social order of the Roman empire, West and East, is possible because of the destruction of old ways of being, old ways of interacting. Viewed synchronically, that is at any given moment in time, the ancient community requires a scapegoat to help establish a boundary between inside and outside, inclusion and exclusion. It finds that scapegoat, as we saw in chapter 1, in the recurrent figure of the tyrant, who, not surprisingly, populates the pages of declamation and the imagination of rhetorically influenced writers of prose and poetry right down through the end of the classical world. But the later world of Greece and Rome requires a scapegoat as well, to mark the historical transition from a system of free city-states to the more harmonious if in any many ways more constraining cultures of Hellenism and Romanism. It finds such scapegoats in Demosthenes and Cicero, respectively, two figures who are forever honored and forever debased by the traditions that keep their memories and their influence alive. They become foundation sacrifices for the unifying culture of Greco-Roman rhetoric, and killing them, if only through speech, constitutes an important stage in each generation's rite of passage into rhetorical culture. From the crucible of rhetorical training and competition emerges the transformed, or newly formed, elite male subject, possessed of a distinctive linguistic, sexual, political, and intellectual identity, an identity that for all of its fragility and artificiality maintains a powerful hold on the imagination of Greco-Roman civilization and its successor phases of culture in the Mediterranean world and beyond.

5

The Afterlife of Rhetoric

Already in antiquity the effects of rhetoric are observable beyond the immediate contexts of the school, the forum, and the public assembly. Rhetorical education transformed the student into more than just the master of a craft: it affected his sense of self, his political identity, his approach to all aspects of life, private as well as public. At the same time, as systematic training in the effective use of language, rhetoric, through its former students, shaped virtually every other classical literary genre, and either indirectly, through imitation of the classics, or directly, during revivals of classical rhetorical training, shaped much of later literature as well. So pervasive is the effect of rhetoric since its original efflorescence in the ancient Greek and Roman city-states that it can be difficult to imagine an outside from which to observe the inside of rhetorical culture. But imagine we must if we are to grasp what is at stake in the periodic rejections and revivals of rhetoric.

A key figure in understanding the broader impact of rhetoric is the fourth century BC Athenian writer Isocrates. We have already been introduced to Isocrates through Socrates' complimentary reference to him at the end of Plato's *Phaedrus*. There, Socrates contrasts the well-born Isocrates with the mere craftsman and resident alien Lysias. The compliment – like most Socratic compliments – has an edge to it, since Isocrates himself, having seen his family's fortune diminished in the Peloponnesian War, briefly worked as a logographos, or writer of speeches for others, just like Lysias. But unlike Lysias, Isocrates was able to parlay that experience, as well as his training under none other than Gorgias, into a position as teacher of elite youth and adviser to all of Athens, indeed all of Greece and the Greek-speaking world, on matters of grave import. Isocrates numbers among his students the

Athenian general Timotheus, whom he praises at length in a speech composed near the end of his own life (*Antidosis*), as well as the orators Isaeus, Lycurgus, and Hyperides (three of the canonical ten Attic orators: not a bad percentage), the historians Ephorus and Theopompus, and the philosopher Speusippus, who after Plato's death succeeded him as head of the Academy. And Isocrates' surviving writings are addressed variously to a Cyprian king, to Philip of Macedon, to the Athenian assembly, and, most importantly, to all literate Greeks. In an autobiographical passage Isocrates reports that he opted to exercise influence through writing and through the teaching of small, but potentially influential groups of young men due to "a smallness of voice" (*mikrophônia*) from which he suffered – a claim that has been plausibly interpreted as less a comment on Isocrates' physiognomy than a rejection of the brawling politics of the Athenian assembly where "loudmouths" were by Isocrates' time thought to dominate.

Partly due to his privileged social position as a free citizen of free and democratic Athens, Isocrates was able to reconceptualize rhetoric, presenting it not only as a craft for shaping an immediate context, but also as an education in citizenship. Whereas Gorgias and other sophists provided (among other things) a useful vocational training and important skill for functioning in a democratic setting, Isocrates appears from his own account to be almost a prototype of a modern professor of political science or cultural studies or communication. On the one hand, he acknowledges the narrowly practical value of training in the craft of rhetoric; on the other, he suggests that orderly deliberation and reflection in a context removed from the passions of the courtroom or the assembly is more likely to generate wise advice on policy than are the actual processes of political debate.

To some, in antiquity as in succeeding generations, this combination of removal from the public sphere with insistence on shaping policy bespeaks a rejection of democracy and, in effect, a legitimation of oligarchy, albeit an oligarchy based on intelligence and training, and not necessarily wealth and military power. And, to be sure, much of the actual advice that Isocrates offers in his writings on the urgent questions of his day inclines towards conservation of existing structures and institutions internally and collaboration with Macedon in external affairs. But it can also be argued that Isocrates' approach to rhetoric, not to mention his approach to pressing political questions, contributes to democratic culture in the long run, in that he seeks to educate citizens who speak not from their own particular vantage point but from their best sense of the long-term interests of the community. As we saw in our brief discussion of Demosthenes' speech *On Behalf of the Megalopolitans*, the context of public oratory required the speaker to present himself as acting on behalf of the polis as a whole. Isocrates' claim is that through his teaching and writing the student and/or reader can discern the civic interest in any given situation. Unlike Aristotle, who accepts that rhetoric is the art of finding the most effective means of persuasion and thus seeks to systematize its study and presentation, Isocrates makes of rhetoric a collaborative process of deliberation, one that claims to produce both sound political judgment and trustworthy political agents.

There is historical irony in the fact that the philosopher Aristotle composed a famous treatise on rhetoric, while the rhetorician Isocrates tended to shy away from association with the very term rhetoric. But Isocrates' self-identification as a teacher of philosophy and as a proponent of the power of logos, or reasoning expressed in language, does not change the fact that of the two great fourth century BC thinkers, it is Isocrates, not Aristotle, who provided the rationale for rhetoric to serve as the preeminent mode of acculturation in antiquity, and Isocrates, not Aristotle, who by his own example established rhetoric as an approach to written as well as oral discourse. Isocrates did not wish to be identified as a rhetor because of the contemporary association of rhetorical training with self-interested cunning in the use of language. But this terminological reticence did not keep later writers, thinkers, and educators from following his example and repeating his arguments in their steadfast association of rhetorical education with the formation of responsible political subjects. Both politically, in his clear articulation of the relationship between rhetoric and the state, and technologically, in his demonstration of the adaptability of rhetoric to writing as well as speaking, Isocrates makes possible the persistent impact of rhetoric well beyond the context of its own creation.

Two passages give further insight into Isocrates' aims and impact. First, in a work written in the persona of the Cyprian king Nicocles, Isocrates asserts "the practice of making speeches" is "of all faculties inborn in human beings the one responsible for the most that is good" (*Nicocles* 5). It is speech that makes us superior to other living creatures, and it is through "our inborn capacity to persuade one another and to make clear to ourselves that which we deem advisable, that we not only abandon our animal existence but also in joining together found cities and establish laws and invent arts. Indeed, speech has been a partner in fashioning virtually everything that we have devised" (*Nicocles* 6). As the repetition of the first person plural of the verb, as well as of the prefix *syn-*, meaning "together," makes clear in the original Greek, Isocrates construes eloquence as a social endeavor. So far, then, he is in accord with his teachers the sophists and with the institutions of the Athenian democracy. Indeed, he suggests, "if it were not for principles of justice and injustice, of baseness and honorability established by eloquence, we would not be able to live with one another" (*Nicocles* 7). In short, eloquence constructs the moral as well as the social order.

This reference to morality as established by eloquence, while reinforcing the sophistic claim that "man is the measure of all things," also permits Isocrates to consider the relationship of eloquence to individual character. And so he proceeds to argue that through the faculty of speech we "contend about doubtful matters and investigate together about those which are unknown, for with the very proofs through which we persuade others we also take counsel with ourselves, and while we call those men eloquent who are able to speak before the demos, we consider sagacious [Greek, *eubouloi*] those who examine matters most skillfully on their own" (*Nicocles* 8). Without quite abandoning the social dimension of eloquence – as evidenced by the repeated use of "we" – Isocrates has turned it into an external marker of an internal character trait. At one level he is defending himself and his students against charges of quietism, suggesting that thoughtful deliberation is an aspect of rhetoric, not a rival to it. But he is also opening the door to the use of rhetoric to structure and inform written communication as well, since writing in antiquity tended to be seen as a private endeavor, a mark of secrecy, even of tyrannical isolation from and disdain for the life of the community. Instead, Isocrates suggests, in a written treatise made to seem like the oral pronouncement of a king to his people, writing is just the quiet interior to speechmaking's boisterous exterior: skill in one implies skill in the other. "In all of our actions and in all of our thoughts, speech is our guide. And those who have the most good sense are the ones who use speech the most" (*Nicocles* 9).

In a passage from the *Panathenaicus*, a work composed while he was in his nineties, Isocrates expatiates on the qualities to be found in a well-educated person, that is to say, one who has undergone the

Isocratean training in logos. The passage seems to describe personal characteristics, that is, aspects of everyday action and deportment, yet it is clear that these characteristics are closely aligned with the special capacities of the successful orator:

> Whom then do I call educated . . . ? First, those who make good use of the circumstances they encounter day by day, who possess a judgment that can match the occasion and hit upon the expedient course of action. Next, those who behave appropriately and justly toward all with whom they associate, bearing in a good-natured and easy-going manner the obnoxious behavior of others while making themselves as inoffensive and even-tempered as possible. Third, those who always regulate their pleasures, not letting themselves be overcome by misfortune but instead dealing with it in a manly way as befits our shared nature. Fourth, and most important, those who are not spoiled by success, who don't abandon their old selves or become overbearing, but remain steadfast in the ranks of clear thinkers. (Isocrates, *Panathenaic Oration* 30–2)

It is hard to tell from reading the passage whether Isocrates is describing a good man, a good citizen, or a good orator. Such indeterminability is precisely the point. Interiority and exteriority are two sides of the same coin, in Isocrates' view, as are the personal and the political, the written and the oral, and so forth. Isocrates' claim is not about privileging one side of a dichotomy over another, or viewing one as subsidiary to the other: both sides of the polarities public–private, interior–exterior, personal–political, written–oral manifest the same rhetorical impulse to "match the occasion." Thus, without denying the close association of rhetoric with the state, and in particular with the ancient city-state, Isocrates' account of eloquence makes possible its transferability to radically new contexts in the ancient world and beyond.

As already intimated, one such context newly and repeatedly animated by rhetoric is the composition of written literature. Although most literature in antiquity was composed to be performed in some social context, and thus does not entail the radical sense of interiority inspired by later monastic habits of encountering written texts, nevertheless, as writing, it reached audiences at a remove in time and space, in contrast to the immediacy of the encounter with speechmaking and declamation. Despite this difference in reception, the written genres of ancient Greek and Latin literature quickly fell under the sway of rhetorical principles of invention, arrangement, and style. In part this development was due to the education of the authors in question, from the Greek historians who trained with Isocrates to the Roman poets such as Ovid and Lucan who spent their youth – and possibly a good portion of their adulthood – in the schools of the declaimers. But it is also the case that writers of genres ranging from epic to history to love poetry to satire to philosophy found in rhetoric a way to encourage the reanimation of the spoken voice in each and every subsequent encounter with a text. Few and far between were the ancient writers who regarded writing as an end in itself. Instead, it was an aid for memory, a prompt for performance, a libretto, as it were, to be brought to life through the voice of the reader – whether that reader was the poet himself, a professional reciter, or an individual listening to the sound of his or her interior voice. Indeed, in the first passage from Isocrates quoted above, when he imagines interior deliberation he describes the deliberating subject as carrying on a conversation or dialogue (*dialexis*) with himself. In so doing, Isocrates presupposes the ordinary conditions under which an individual reader would experience writing.

Failure to acknowledge the function of writing as prompt for performance has led to wrong-headed criticism of much post-Isocratean literature as overly rhetorical. Later critics seem particularly surprised by the extent to which prose genres, such as history and philosophy, sound as if written to be declaimed. But it is really no surprise at all, given Isocrates' demonstration of the interdependence of voice and text, that his pupils and successors should write in a style that draws upon rhetoric's systematic instruction in the adaptation of the voice to the pressures of circumstance, subject matter, and audience – whether that audience is construed as immediate and present or removed in time and space. It is conventional to ascribe the moralizing tone and fondness for character sketch found in the works of ancient historians, starting with Ephorus and Theopompus, to their rhetorical background. Perhaps equally rhetorical is the deep-seated sense of history as a human creation: not a series of events that happened, but a compendium of choices made badly or well under contingent circumstances. Indeed, the relationship between the declamatory exercises known as suasoriae (see chapter 4, above) and historiography is something of a chicken-and-egg problem: did the popularity of the rhetorical exercise lead to the inclusion of dramatic scenes of choice and advice in ancient history writing, or was it the other way around? Certainly, in the Roman case, it can be established both that the historian Livy was influenced by rhetorical practices and that he in turn influenced the practice of rhetoric. In a similar vein, philosophy, while never losing its fondness for subtle disputation or Aristotelian analysis, as a literary genre comes to privilege the voice of persuasion. We encounter this voice in authors as disparate as the Greek philosopher Epicurus, who exhorts his followers through his letters, and the Roman statesman Cicero, who in the person of one dead aristocrat after another holds forth for his readers exempla of proper aristocratic behavior. Especially memorable is the case of Seneca the Younger, who in his letters on moral topics seeks to update the literary personae of both Epicurus and Cicero and, more generally, in a diverse and abundant series of philosophical treatises publicizes an array of internal moral dramas, replete with interlocutors, counter-arguments, altercations, character sketches, narrations, and most noticeably sharp and pointed sententiae – all of which he was as likely to have learned from his teachers of rhetoric as from his predecessors in the Stoic philosophical sect.

The impact of rhetoric on poetry is enormous as well. Traces of rhetorical style are evident in contemporary poetry as soon as there is rhetorical practice to speak of: thus the agones, or debates, that formed a crucial part of the fifth-century BC tragedian Euripides' dramaturgical practice would have invited comparison to the form and content of contemporary deliberative and forensic speeches, while the Roman playwright Plautus engaged in pitch-perfect parody of the aristocratic braggadocio that forms an important part of early Roman speechmaking. It is sometimes said that Roman poetry becomes more rhetorical with the passage from the republic to the empire, either as a general sign of decline or as part of a greater interest in surface as opposed to depth. Actually, it is more accurate to say that Roman literature becomes more sententious over time, as authors in all genres strive to create memorable tag-lines as their own contribution to a growing and less easily managed patrimony of received wisdom. Moreover, as the social importance of rhetoric as a medium of geographical or class mobility increases under the Roman empire, rhetoric and rhetorical education understandably become themes of discussion and topics of analysis, especially for authors of a satiric bent. Thus a key figure in Petronius' *Satyricon*, a picaresque novel about young men who struggle to make the transition to full civic (and sexual) adulthood, is the self-pitying teacher of rhetoric Agamemnon. And the satirist Juvenal simultaneously ridicules and reinforces rhetorical exercises on common theses – should a man marry? is this generation worse than the preceding? – by producing hilarious verse satires thereon. Rhetorical culture is the world in which these and other writers dwell, and they reveal their possession of "judgment that matches the occasion" precisely by addressing the circumstances of their own place in literary and cultural history.

Making the most of the occasion – an ideal summed up in the Greek word *kairos* – is a concept that runs all through the ancient rhetorical tradition and ramifies in ways that scholars have only slowly come to recognize. Certainly, the precedent of Gorgias was crucial in making kairos a keyword of the ancient rhetorical tradition. He wrote a treatise on kairos in which, it would seem, he argued that it was necessary to study rhetoric scientifically in order to be prepared to adapt to circumstances as they presented themselves. He spoke of not missing an opportunity (*ton kairon mê diamartein*), of harmonizing one's language with the occasion. In a sense, then, the principle of kairos encapsulates the notion of rhetoric as socially constructive, only it imagines the rhetor as working in harmony with all that the occasion provides: his training, the resources of language, the state of mind of the audience, the circumstances of the speech, surrounding events, and so on. The reference to harmony is not accidental, since kairos is also a musical term, describing the convergence in a single moment of sounds made by different instruments, including the human voice. To speak of the kairos of the rhetorician is thus to turn his performance into both an aesthetic and a scientific achievement.

One way of understanding the emphasis on kairos in the works of Gorgias and his followers, including Isocrates, is to see in it an acknowledgment of the inaccessibility of truth and thus of the inevitability of immersion in the world of opinion or *doxa*. This may well be the case, but it does not mean that a privileging of kairos in and of itself necessarily implies a relativist or skeptical epistemology. Indeed, it has recently been suggested that key elements of early Christian thought can be understood as the application of classical rhetorical concepts, chief among them kairos and pistis, to a Hebrew religious tradition that emphasized confidence in a communal and personal relationship with a supreme being. Certainly, the opening of the Gospel of John invites such an interpretation: if the God of the Torah identifies himself through a series of statements involving forms of the verb "to be" (e.g., "I am the God of your forefathers," "I am who I am"), then one way of explaining his relationship to the person of Jesus Christ is to call Jesus the "logos," that is the Word, of God. To a rhetorically trained Greek-speaking audience (i.e., one audience for much of early Christian scripture, regardless of ethnicity), the phrase "In the beginning was the word and the word was with God," etc., is an announcement of the inseparability of Father and Son, of Being and Language. Jesus becomes the intrinsically human means through which divine being comes to be known.

But if the Word has been with God from the beginning, then what is the sense of a story about a God-man who lives one human life at a specific time and place? Here the concept of kairos comes into play, suggesting not that Jesus is an emanation from the world of opinion, but that he is the right expression of the word for the occasion. The story told of him is true, but it is not complete (indeed, John stresses its incompleteness in the final words of the gospel, declaring: "And there are many other things that Jesus did; if all were written down, I think the universe itself does not have room for the books that would be written," 21.25). It is an expression of kairos that allows for the possibility of other kairotic encounters with God under other circumstances. Indeed, in recent theology the ancient rhetorical notion of kairos has itself been adapted to present circumstances as a way of explaining the paradox of change in church doctrine over time. On this view, it is not God's truth that has changed, when for example, the church becomes more accepting of equality between men and women; rather, its kairotic encounter with the particular circumstances in which it is being proclaimed and heard leads to an appearance of variation. Acceptance of the principle of kairos thus allows the believer to modify beliefs without thereby repudiating his or her own prior experience.

Connected to such meditations on kairos as both historical explanation and principle of communal transformation is the additional historical claim that the very notion of Christian faith is also derived in part from ancient rhetoric. Hebrew scripture never doubts the existence of God: faith is confidence in the supreme being, not belief that he exists. Faith is thus a spiritual or emotional experience, not an intellectual one. In Greek philosophy, of course, exactly the opposite is true: much of the point of the intellectual askesis of philosophy is to rid the subject of attachment to false beliefs due to the intrusion of the passions. While ascent to the Platonic forms, for example, may be propelled by desire (as in Plato's *Symposium*), the key steps are intellectual in nature and the ultimate engagement with the forms is through contemplation and knowledge, not feeling. Christian faith is different from both. It is belief *that* (i.e., it has a propositional content) as well as belief *in*. The Greek rhetorical term *pistis*, which is used by the writers of the New Testament as well as the early Church Fathers, nicely combines the two in that it refers to both the process and the end result of persuasion. That the early Christian writings were composed in Greek for an audience that would be familiar with rhetoric as the structuring principle of political life in Hellenized Palestine (and later, the rest of the Roman empire) makes the case for rhetorical influence on the conceptualization of Christian faith more substantial. Whether they understood early church history in this way or not, Christian polemicists of the Reformation and Counter-Reformation seem to have repeated the early reliance on classical rhetoric as a basis for articulating principles of Christian doctrine. Writers like Melanchthon and Luther, on the one hand, and their Catholic opponents on the other, drew on both Latin and Greek rhetorical terminology (e.g., *persuasio*, *fides*, in addition to *pistis*) to stake out conflicting views on, for example, the relative importance of conviction versus assent in the Christian experience of faith. Protestant writers in particular struggled with the tension between their view of God as speaking directly to his people and their own immediate need to win converts to their point of view. The latter concern in part – but only in part – explains Luther's insistence that rhetoric was the most important topic to be treated in a Faculty of Arts.

If early Christians drew on Greek rhetoric to articulate key aspects of their new system of belief, equally did they employ rhetoric instrumentally as a means of securing the identity of their emergent community and advancing its interests. By displaying their rhetorical education, Christians such as John Chrysostom, Gregory of Nazianzus, and Basil of Caesarea seek to legitimize Christian discourse in the eyes of hostile pagan elites, while at the same time reinforcing belief within the Christian community, especially through their preaching. As George Kennedy writes, "they were concerned with moving the hearts of their audience and inspiring their lives, and the devices of sophistic rhetoric had become the cues to which their audiences responded and by which their purposes could be best accomplished."[1]

In the Western portion of the Roman empire, Augustine of Hippo becomes the primary exponent of the adaptability of classical rhetoric to the spread of Christian doctrine and exhortation to Christian practice. His great treatise, *City of God*, even in its title assimilates Christianity to the political context that prompted the creation of classical rhetoric. And in the fourth book of his work *On Christian Doctrine* (*De Doctrina Christiana*) Augustine expatiates on the usefulness of rhetoric for the Christian mission of interpretation and promulgation of the word of God. Preachers and teachers like Augustine come to assume a combined function comparable to that of orators and rhetoricians in the classical tradition. They articulate the consensus of the community while actively suppressing what they regard as heresy (i.e., wrong teaching and misguided practices based upon them). Where they crucially differ from the classical rhetoricians is in their conviction that there is in fact a truth that has already been revealed, namely the truth of scripture. Their task is to interpret scripture, persuasively and efficaciously (i.e., rhetorically). But they are never more than interpreters of revelation and in that respect comparable to the poet-prophets whom the classical rhetoricians replaced. As a consequence, the Church Fathers cannot regard rhetoric as a craft in quite the same sense as the classical orators and rhetoricians. For the pagan writers and speakers, it will be recalled, the craft of rhetoric fashioned the truth; for the Christians, as Augustine makes abundantly clear, it located and communicated the truth revealed in scripture. As he puts it, "There are two things upon which every treatment of the scriptures depends: the means of discovering what the thought may be, and the means of expressing what the thought is" (*On Christian Doctrine* 4.1). In Augustine's version of classical rhetoric, discovery, or invention, is no longer the creation of arguments or the identification of the best means of persuasion in the matter at hand, but the discovery of the truth of scripture. And the rest of rhetoric (in his case, style, memory, and performance) considers the means through which that truth might be conveyed to a given audience. In effect, then, it is the Christian writers, much more than their pagan counterparts, who disseminate the view that style is an elective means of communicating a substance that is always already there. For the Christian, rhetoric can be a useful aspect of acculturation into an interpretive elite, but never a criterion for membership in the communion of saints.

It will take the recreation of the secular state in the early modern period for rhetoric to move again to the center of political and social life. The early humanists' revival of Greek and Latin learning – exemplified for us by Poggio Bracciolini's discovery of the manuscript of Quintilian in a storeroom at the monastery of St. Gall in 1416 – was prompted in part by a desire to bring to expression a secular political and social consciousness latent within medieval Catholicism. For the humanists, the classical struggle between rhetoric and philosophy could be read as a prototype of their own attempt to dislodge scholasticism as the dominant intellectual mode of the late medieval period. The revival of classical rhetoric spread quickly during the fifteenth and sixteenth centuries under humanist leadership and took hold in a variety of settings, from Protestant England, to Catholic France, Spain, and Poland, to Orthodox Russia (although there a more direct relationship with the Byzantine heirs to the classical tradition was also relevant). Rhetoric was in no sense hostile to church teaching and in fact was perfectly capable of serving the forces of sectarianism, as evidence by the writings of Luther, Calvin, More, Borromeo, Loyola, and others. But it also provided a shared discourse for a new leadership class within and among emerging capitalist nation-states. The adaptability of rhetoric to both oral and written contexts pioneered by key ancient figures such as Isocrates and Cicero proved handy in the early modern period as well. At times the student of rhetoric imagines himself a versatile courtier, responding on the spot to the personal and political challenges of face-to-face contexts, such as the monarch's court or a newly powerful parliament. As such he may play up the social elitism of the classical tradition, a tendency well illustrated by the Italian writer Castiglione's *Book of the Courtier*. This branch of humanist and early modern rhetoric is often associated with the Italian term *sprezzatura* – a personal versatility and responsiveness to the immediacy of the situation. Sprezzatura is something of a distant heir of Greek kairos, only without the profound epistemological and social consequences of the sophistic term. Indeed, writings on sprezzatura, or on rhetorical performance more generally, often emphasize, in contrast to the Greek tradition, the unteachability of rhetorical versatility. Rhetoric thus becomes a cover for a certain kind of aristocratic privilege represented as inaccessible to the lower orders.

But as with classical rhetoric, so with its humanist and early modern revival, a democratizing strain is visible as well. The sheer number of treatises gives us some sense of the proliferation of interest: one article on Renaissance rhetoric refers in its title to "One Thousand Neglected Authors."[2] And many of these authors, neglected or not, aimed to instruct the newly empowered merchants and townspeople in the art of presenting their petitions and points of view clearly and persuasively. Indeed, it does not seem an exaggeration to say that the sense of rupture with preceding generations that characterizes the movement known as the Renaissance is, paradoxically, due in part to the rediscovery of rhetoric with its insistence on the possibility of making the world anew through language. As under the Roman empire, so under the newly forming European nations, the essentially oral art of rhetoric comes to be associated as well with the production of texts that circulated through writing and eventually form a literary tradition. Poetry, essays, and dramas (written but of course also performed) built upon rhetoric's power of imagining otherwise and in so doing fostered large-scale but discrete national identities out of the disparate communities of Europe as it emerged from feudalism. Shakespeare, like his queen Elizabeth, was trained in rhetoric (the latter was reckoned by her tutor an especially fine interpreter of Demosthenes). Their England, imagined into being through language – as well as force of arms and confiscations – has more than a little in common with the Sophistopolis of the Greek declaimers, perhaps in particular in its ability to cohere into a self-regenerating ideal.

The nationalism of the early modern period in which new nation-states coalesced around powerful monarchs is of course quite different from the Romantic nationalism that swept through Europe, the Americas, and eventually much of the rest of the world in the after-math of the French Revolution and Napoleonic Wars. In the latter case, bloodlines, real or imagined, often came to serve as the basis for membership within the national community. Language was important, and conflict over the linguistic rights of majorities and minorities still plague nation-states today, but the notion of a national identity formed through the collective deliberation of a rhetorically trained populace fell by the wayside. Paradoxically, the republican forms of government that tended to take shape in later nation-states may have allowed for more immediate and practical uses of rhetoric than did the Tudor and Stuart monarchies or the Bourbon court. But the constitutive power of classical rhetoric and the commitment to versatile response to changing circumstances had little purchase in a world dominated by myths of autochthony and ideals of purity or distinctiveness of blood. The development of such racialized thinking and its gruesome con-sequences are well beyond the scope of this book. Some might see its efficient cause in the French Revolution and subsequent Counter-Revolution and Terror, a sequence of events that has long been understood as, among other things, manifesting a crisis of rhetoric.

Did the Jacobins "electrify" the populace to take arms against an oppressive aristocracy? Or did they "abuse language" out of self-interest?[3] Were they heirs of republican Roman citizen-statesmen – *viri boni dicendi periti* – or the avant-garde of a new imperial order in which the rhetorical tongue yielded to the Napoleonic laurel?

More generally, racist republicanism, with its insistence on the biological basis of community, can be seen as the perverted counter-part of an Enlightenment commitment to disinterested scientific inquiry and privileging of natural science over religious and moral dogma. From this perspective, too, rhetoric was in for a difficult time, losing its hold on the formation of scientific, cultural, and in time, political elites. In a sense, during the eighteenth and nineteenth centuries, rhetoric is virtually squeezed out of existence as anything but a narrowly practical art of public speaking by the twin forces of science and Romanticism. The one considers it irrelevant, the other makes it so. It is during this period, and really only this period, in Western history that rhetoric becomes something of a dirty word, a catchall for shoddy thinking, duplicitous argumentation, useless ornamentation, and the like. Thus it is with some bemusement that the historian of rhetoric observes today as scientists (or their allies in the philosophical com-munity) and scholars of Romanticism alike struggle to revive the lost (to them) lessons of classical rhetoric.

What I call the scientific return to rhetoric is in effect a recognition of the rhetorical dimension of science and of philosophical and other discourses that seek to emulate science. The separation of argument, or more specifically invention, from style, disposition, and perform-ance that characterized the writing of Petrus Ramus in the sixteenth century and Descartes in the seventeenth led to the institutionaliza-tion of scientific inquiry as a sphere of knowledge distinct from other human enterprises. In a sense, experimentation and induction came to occupy the space of invention, and rhetoric was left without an epistemological function. Writing in 1667 of the recent establishment of the British Royal Society, Thomas Sprat records that its members were concerned lest

the whole spirit and vigour of the Design, had soon been eaten out, by the luxury and redundance of speech. The ill effects of this superfluity of talking, have already overwhelm'd most other Arts and Professions; insomuch, that when I consider the means of happy living, and the causes of their corruption, I can hardly forbear . . . concluding, that eloquence ought to be banish'd out of all civil Societies, as a thing fatal to Peace and good Manners.[4]

Luxury, redundance, and superfluity are now conceived of, not as rhetorical virtues, that is as means of constructing a richer and more exhaustive social reality out of language, but as barriers between knowledge and its objects, and thus deleterious to the well-being of communities founded upon reason.

It took scholars working within the traditions of Enlightenment science some three centuries to acknowledge the impossibility of Sprat's ambition to expel eloquence. Not only was eloquence necessary for the ongoing maintenance of human communities, it was also not so easily separated from scientific and philosophical argumentation. Chaim Perelman, who in the mid-twentieth century surveyed instances of argumentation in precisely the professions that interested Sprat (law, philosophy, science), noted that discussion was still structured in accordance with the principles, patterns, and topoi or loci of ancient rhetoric. In effect, science (broadly understood) could be seen to have had a rhetoric all along. Perhaps more surprisingly (at least to the scientific community), Stephen Toulmin argued from within the perspective of science and analytical philosophy that by, in effect, ignoring argument, the two interrelated disciplines had reduced their own ability to tackle real-world problems. Toulmin sought to replace the study of formal logic with careful investigation of practical reasoning as employed across disciplines. For Toulmin, mathematics, which had since at least Descartes served as "the model for formal logicians to analyze," is in fact the odd man out, the only intellectual activity "whose problems and solutions are 'above time.'"[5] In recognizing the time-bound nature of all human argumentation and the formal similarity of arguments across intellectual disciplines (reliance on data and warrants, and specification of modalities, such as "probably," "likely"), Toulmin reinterprets scientific inquiry as, in effect, a human-centered, world-defining rhetorical enterprise. Toulmin's conclusions can now be applied retrospectively to the interrelation of science and rhetoric in the ancient world. It seems quite possible that scholars have been too quick to impose an Enlightenment distinction between science and eloquence on the textual remains of antiquity. After all, Aristotle was both a biologist and an author of a rhetorical treatise, while figures like Cicero and Quintilian recommended familiarity with science and mathematics as part of the training of the orator.

Critical to the twentieth-century reevaluation of rhetoric has been the writing of the late-nineteenth century German philologist and philosopher Friedrich Nietzsche. As an expert in classical Greece and Rome, Nietzsche immersed himself in their rhetorical cultures and delivered a series of lectures on ancient rhetoric as part of his professorial responsibilities at the University of Basel. Nietzsche's lectures closely follow the work of other scholars of his day (a not unparalleled strategy for many a college instructor), but his reflections on rhetoric do not remain limited to transmission of historical knowledge. In particular, the third section of Nietzsche's "Description of Ancient Rhetoric," in which he insists that "the *rhetorical is a further development*, guided by the clear light of the understanding, of *the artistic means which are already found in language*,"[6] reverberates throughout his non-classical writing, in particular in his famous essay "On Truth and Lying in an Extra-Moral Sense." (As a matter of chronology we might note that the lectures on rhetoric were prepared for the winter term 1872–3, while "On Truth and Lying" was composed in 1873.)

The latter essay begins with a remarkable anecdote, one that, in effect, turns on its head the ancient sophists' meditations on the role of human beings in the universe. As Nietzsche writes:

> In some remote corner of the universe that is poured out in countless flickering solar systems, there once was a star on which clever animals invented knowledge. That was the most arrogant and the most untruthful moment in "world history" – yet indeed only a moment. After nature had taken a few breaths, the star froze over and the clever animals had to die.[7]

Apart from reminding us of the relative insignificance of the human species from the vantage point of cosmic time, Nietzsche wants to claim that everything human beings consider truth, inasmuch as it is constituted through human perception and human language, has at best a metaphorical relationship to reality. The "thing-in-itself" (he continues),

> is . . . absolutely incomprehensible to the creator of language and not worth seeking. He designates only the relations of things to men, and to express these relations he uses the boldest metaphors. First, he translates a nerve stimulus into an image! That is the first metaphor.

Then the image must be reshaped into a sound! The second metaphor. And each time there is a complete overleaping of spheres – from one sphere to the center of a totally different one . . . When we speak of trees, colors, snow, and flowers, we believe we know something about the things themselves, although what we have are just metaphors of things, which do not correspond at all to the original entities.[8]

For Nietzsche, then, truth is nothing but the metaphor that sticks. Or rather, "a mobile army of metaphors, metonyms, anthropomorphisms, in short, a sum of human relations which were poetically and rhetorically heightened, transferred, and adorned, and after long use seemed solid, canonical, and binding to a nation."[9] Common parlance identifies as "liar" the individual who "misuses established conventions by arbitrary substitutions and even reversals of names."[10] In fact, on Nietzsche's view, all of us are liars inasmuch as all of us use language to make claims about reality.

Nietzsche, writing in an era when scientific empiricism is ascendant, draws on the resources of ancient rhetoric to construct a deliberately paradoxical view of the relationship between reality and language. Rather than an approximation to reality, language is a metaphorical distancing from it. The only reality language has access to is the social reality it creates. What Nietzsche's contemporaries (and many today) still dismissively call rhetoric is for him the intensification of the metaphorical function (or what he earlier had called "the artistic means") intrinsic to all language. What is more, following the ancient example closely, if not explicitly, Nietzsche sees that the truth constructed by language is a social truth, one that may well vary from community to community, not (and here again he stands in opposition to many of his contemporaries) because of differences of bloodline, but because of differences of language. In his writing on classical rhetoric, Nietzsche even goes so far as to assert that rhetoric is "an essentially *republican* art: one must be accustomed to tolerating the most unusual opinions and points of view . . . one must be just as willing to listen as to speak."[11] Just as he employs classical rhetoric to undercut the triumphalist empiricism and foundationalist epistemologies of his intellectual contemporaries, so too in his assessment of the politics of rhetoric Nietzsche proclaims its republicanism in an era when anti-republican, or Caesarist, models of political authority are still being aggressively championed in Prussia, France, Russia, Latin America, and elsewhere.[12] If, in his anecdote about the "clever

animals" who invented knowledge, Nietzsche shows us that the
Protagorean declaration of "human being as the measure of all things"
is a humbling as well as a liberating recognition, nonetheless he seems
to acknowledge, even relish, the anti-authoritarianism implicit in the
rhetorical practices founded by the ancients.

Nietzsche's insistence on the metaphorical or rhetorical nature of
all language opens the floodgates for twentieth-century intellectual
movements that seek to privilege rhetoric at the expense of philosophy. A diverse range of influential thinkers, from Heidegger to
Foucault, Lacan, and Derrida, draws explicitly or implicitly on
Nietzsche's rhetorical approach to language. Some might go so far as
to describe literary theory as the true heir to ancient rhetoric in the
modern world. But there is a crucial difference between, say, Derrida,
and Nietzsche, especially in the passages just discussed, that locates
Nietzsche much closer to the ancients than to his modern successors.
For what has happened with figures like Derrida and Lacan in particular is that language has been detached, not just from its referents
(a move we can easily see Nietzsche making as well), but also from
the situation and intent of its producers. For Lacan, the human
subject is constituted in and through language. Human language
precedes the human being, the human being enters a world of language that is always already there. For Derrida, as well, "il n'y a pas de
hors-texte" – "there is no beyond-text." Derrida rigorously applies
Nietzsche's insight concerning the unknowability of the world through
language in order to criticize a range of activities, analytical philosophy foremost among them, that in his view take such knowability
for granted. For Derrida, the search, through language, for the impossible knowledge of what lies beyond, manifests itself in (among other
things) a persistent privileging of speech over writing, as if speech
were somehow closer to what it signifies than writing is. Reversing
this traditional privileging, Derrida attends to the self-evidently artificial aspects of writing as a means of deconstructing the constructed
relationship between language and reality.

In certain ways, then, Derrida seems very much in accord with
the spirit of ancient rhetoric – in, for example, his insistence on the
constructedness of philosophical "truth," in his attention to the
artificiality of the texts he analyzes, and in the deliberateness of his
own practice as a writer. But his privileging of writing over speaking,
while not ipso facto anti-rhetorical (Isocrates and Cicero had shown
the way to a written rhetoric, we will recall), does seem to neglect or

deemphasize the social aspect of rhetoric, both the willingness to speak and to listen referred to by Nietzsche and the broader acceptance of others' right to power built into the daily practice of the ancient city-state. This is not to say that writing is not a social practice; rather, that the privileging of orality rejected by Derrida has as its historical wellspring not just a "metaphysics of presence," but also an active concern with sociability. Ancient rhetoric – and here I think Nietzsche in making the creators of language and truth plural has got it exactly right – is concerned with knowledge, power, authority, etc., not just as constructed but as *socially* constructed. Gorgias' delivery of speeches on opposite sides of the same topic on successive days, in addition to displaying his virtuosity, invited the audience into the process of decision-making. The rhetorical ideal of kairos was an attempt to theorize the contingency of a given situation, of the possibility that what seemed right (appropriate, true, advisable) in one context might not in another. And as the lore of the rhetoric school made clear, adaptability to situation, including the reaction of audience and competitors, was of the essence of oratorical success. Ancient rhetoric fully acknowledges the gap between language and referent. But it also fully acknowledges – and explores – the connection between speaker and speaker, speaker and audience, writer and reader, reader and reader. The subjects of ancient rhetoric are constituted in and through language, but this constitution in no way deprives them of their role and responsibility as social actors.

The social aspect of rhetoric is the focus of yet another contemporary movement that has direct links to the classical tradition. Unlike literary theory, which, given its privileged position in certain sectors of the academy, might be seen as reanimating classical rhetoric's social elitism, attempts to relate rhetoric to the teaching of composition, both oral and written, have increasingly come to stress the democratic epistemology implicit in the rhetorical tradition. For example, the historian Hayden White has argued for reinstitution of rhetorical education on a mass basis. On his analysis, starting in the early nineteenth century rhetorical training was denied to the masses of students even as education broadened with the rise of industrial capitalism because social elites had no interest in giving lower-status students access to the power of rhetorical language. A return to rhetoric would, in White's view, demonstrate (*à la* Nietzsche) the figurative dimension of all language. Neither rhetorical language nor poetic language would any longer seem unteachable, mysterious, or superfluous. Both would be understood as the intensification of the figurative potential of all language – in other words, as an intensification of the language students and others use on an everyday basis anyway. For White, the political effect of rhetorical training would be largely defensive, allowing students "to comprehend what is really going on, both on and beneath the surfaces, not only in literary discourse but in the peculiar kind of exercise in repression and sublimation that we call merely literate writing."[13]

For other modern-day rhetoricians involved in the day-to-day teaching of composition, rhetorical training, in addition to preparing students to "read" as well as "receive" (White's distinction) messages from the powers-that-be, might also prepare them to constitute new messages through collaborative or collective effort. Such scholars and teachers emphasize the tactical nature of rhetoric, the kairotic encounter with the particularities of a situation. And they insist that rhetorical tactics can be productive as well as critical. "Whereas critical tactics break down oppressive discourses, productive tactics construct communal, democratic, participatory discourses, providing a necessary base from which critique can proceed."[14] For this self-proclaimed "neo-sophistic" approach to writing and speaking, rhetoric is less about charismatic orators or prestigious writers than it is about the cultivation and interaction of large numbers of rhetorically empowered political agents – male as well as female, high status and low. Yet even the competitive dimension of ancient rhetoric is redeemable on this view, since it teaches the student to develop "discourse able to withstand the scrutiny of public contest."[15]

The contemporary revival of rhetoric thus coincides with a revival of interest in democracy as both an old and a new ideal. In contrast to some theorists of democracy, such as Jürgen Habermas and his followers, who seek to construct a "pragmatics of discourse" that will overcome the specificity of the rhetorical moment and its participants and generate instead "universalizable" principles, democratic theorists who have been steeped in the rhetorical tradition place special emphasis on the ability of rhetorical communication to respect both the particular and the universal. For some, the goal of a revival of rhetoric is, as already intimated, to critique and resist universalizing claims made by those with disproportionate power; for others, it is to create conditions of public discourse that will generate trust among participants where it is otherwise lacking. For still others, such as Karl Löwith and Hans Herbert Kögler, the greatest contribution of rhetoric to democratic politics seems to be its capacity to generate self-critique on the part of each speaker, each citizen, each participant in political conversation. As Kögler puts it, citing Löwith, "Only in conversation does the certain basis of one's own discourse freely experience uncertainty through the encounter with the discourse of another, and this experience is not replaceable through any kind of self-examination or self-critique."[16] We might imagine revitalized political discourse – whatever the context – as a large-scale conversation in which, by "talking to strangers" (to borrow Danielle Allen's phrase), we come to understand and trust each other and thereby create the conditions through which the world (or some small part of it) can be made anew.

The days of the ancient city-state are long gone, but if we are to believe the evolutionists cited near the opening of this book, the need for special speech will always be with us. Rhetoric, the special speech of the classical polis, found a home in the formation and maintenance of modern nation-states as well. It allowed the Renaissance humanists to imagine into being secular, transhistorical communities held together by a shared elite discourse. If later nation-builders sought to limit access to rhetoric by hiding it in the humanities curriculum of elite colleges and belittling it as superfluous speech, it was precisely because they recognized its power. Imagine the changes that would come about if every member of the community were truly a "craftsman of persuasion" (*tes peithous demiourgos*: Plato, *Gorgias* 453A). But inasmuch as all language – as Nietzsche, and the bulk of the classical tradition before him, saw – is potentially rhetorical, there is no easy way to eliminate rhetoric without eliminating speech. Which returns us to the anecdote of the origin of rhetoric from within a community reduced to silence by the dictates of the tyrant.

The silence of the Sicilians corresponded to a moment of political and social transformation. It was a silence of fear, but also of ripeness. Some would argue that we face just such a moment of transformation today, as the centuries-old system of nation-states shows signs of wear, and new entities, new identities, lay claim to allegiances around the globe. If we could be silent for just a moment, what would we hear? Certainly, speech exercises its twin capacities for deceit and for imagining otherwise as energetically today as ever before. All around us the slashing effects of everyday language make themselves apparent. What rituals of language are capable of holding our communities together? Will they allow for the possibility of collective construction of a better world? Will they contain within themselves mechanisms of self-criticism, of testing through competition? Or will we – have we – returned to the unchallengeable pronouncements of soothsayers and oracles? Do we rely on messengers bringing knowledge from afar? Can we bring ourselves to be clever animals? Or do we sit in silence, dumb spectators in the theater of life?

So much is at stake in the history of rhetoric.

The history of rhetoric has just begun.

A Brief Outline of Ancient Rhetoric

Parts of Rhetoric

These form the subdivisions of the rhetorical curriculum and mark the stages in preparation and delivery of an oration.

invention (Greek *heuresis*, Latin *inventio*) The discovery of arguments and strategies appropriate to subject matter and context. Includes consideration of stance toward matter at hand and selection of topics, both particular and common, for amplification.

arrangement (Greek *taxis*, Latin *dispositio*) The disposition of arguments, topics, emotional appeals, etc., within a speech or case. Includes study of the conventional order of parts of a speech.

style (Greek *lexis*, Latin *elocutio*) The transformation of arguments and strategies into language. Study and deployment of the resources of the Greek and Latin language appropriate for use under the particular circumstances of performance. Analysis of stylistic effects achieved by earlier writers of both prose and poetry.

memory   (Greek *mnêmê*, Latin *memoria*) Memorization of details of the case, contents of the
speech, and, in many instances, the verbatim
language to be used in the speech under
preparation. May also include study of historical and legal precedents for use in discovering arguments. Training of memory
started at an early age. The less a speaker
relied on notes the better.

Performance, delivery   (Greek *hypokrisis*, Latin *pronuntiatio*) Cultivation of voice, gesture, and demeanor
for purpose of presenting the speech (and
speaker) in the most effective light possible.
Could even include tips on grooming and
attire. In the absence of artificial means of
amplification, vocal training was especially
important, and exercises served to develop
stamina. Training in performance overlapped
with the training of actors – a fact that caused
no end of discomfort for teachers of rhetoric
who were concerned to differentiate the
"manly" self-presentation of the orator from
the desire to please others that was thought
to typify the actor.

Types of Oratory

While the contexts for using oratorical training were limitless, generally all speeches were understood to fall into one of the categories
listed below. At the same time, theorists and practitioners recognized
that a speech of one type could draw on aspects of another; for
example, in the course of defending a client against a legal charge, the
orator might praise his origins, or find fault with the character of the
prosecutor.

deliberative   (Greek *symbouleutikon*, Latin *deliberativum*) Speaking (or writing) aimed at persuading an audience
for or against a proposed course of action.

Recommendations on policy and advice on matters of state are characteristic instances of deliberative oratory.

judicial (Greek *dikanikon*, Latin *forense*) As the name indicates, speeches delivered in the context of trials. Oratory used to analyze a point of law or its applicability to a given situation, or to argue a point as if it were a matter of law.

demonstrative The terminology is more complex than for the other categories of speechmaking. *Demonstrativum genus* is a Latin expression for a type of speaking that aims to demonstrate either the good or the bad features of the subject under consideration. Greek generally did not use an umbrella term. The Greek for a speech of praise is *epideiktikos logos*, hence the adjective "epideictic." A speech of blame was called *psogos*. Latin used *laudatio* as the general term for a speech of praise, building on its early application to funeral oration, and *vituperatio* for a speech of blame. Praise or blame might be directed toward an individual person, a group of people, a city, a mythological character, even an abstract entity.

Modes of Persuasion

Aristotle describes proofs (Greek *pisteis*, Latin *argumenta* or *probationes*) as unartistic (i.e., given to, not found by, the orator, such as testimony and documents) and artistic (discovered by the orator). The artistic proofs fall into three categories.

ethos Proofs based upon the character of the accused, the accuser, the witnesses, and the speaker. These proofs may be explicit or implicit.

logos Proofs based upon reasoning, analysis, argument, as contained in the language of the speaker.

pathos "Proofs" based upon the emotion of the audience as constructed by the speaker.

Stances Toward A Case

The Greek word *stasis* and the Latin *status*, both often translated as "issue," in fact mean "standing" or "stance." Although most easily explained in relationship to judicial oratory, the stances or issues are relevant to demonstrative and deliberative speeches as well. Consideration of stasis requires the orator to decide the overall approach to a case or part of a case by determining the contested issues. Core issues are:

conjecture   Did it happen?

definition   Does it fit the charge?

quality   Is there an aspect of what happened that is exculpatory or that disqualifies it from the charge?

transference   Was it the fault of someone else, either directly or indirectly?

Others added over time include:

intent   Did the accused intend the outcome? What is the relationship between the language and the intent of the law?

conflict of law   Is more than one statute relevant to the case? If so, how to negotiate between them?

equity   Does the law as written and interpreted correspond to a general sense of equity or fairness?

syllogism   Perhaps the case is of such a sort that it could not have been imagined by those who wrote the law. It fits neither the letter nor the intent, narrowly conceived. Might it be regarded as fitting an implicit, broader intent on the part of the lawgiver?

ambiguity   Is the law being applied to the case ambiguous?

Topics

Topics (Greek *topoi*, Latin *loci*) are the "places" to look for arguments, or, as they are called in Lausberg's *Handbook*, "search formulae." Thus, in preparing an epideictic oration, the speaker will look for good things to say about descent, education, wealth, friendships, physical attributes, moral qualities, etc., of the subject being praised. A deliberative speaker will consider the relationship of the proposed policy to security and to honor, with each one subdivided into various components. But it is also clear that certain topics can be applied to a variety of contexts, indeed can be used to expand the frame of reference of a particular case. These broader topics are known as *loci communes*. Sometimes they describe logical extensions of the subject under consideration; other times they attempt to sway the audience by relating the case to familiar prejudices and stereotypes. Some familiar *loci communes* include:

- attacks on the morals of the age
- denunciation of luxury
- denunciation of adultery
- praise (or denunciation) of marriage, of childrearing, of childlessness
- praise of the countryside
- denunciation of the city
- lamentation for the brevity of life, the unpredictability of fortune, the cruelty of tyrants
- denunciation (or praise) of the reliability of witnesses, of testimony given under torture, of the value of rumors

Figures of Thought, Figures of Language, and Tropes

Not always clearly differentiated, figures of thought (Greek *skhêmata dianoias*, Latin *figurae sententiae*) involve a structuring of the relationship of speaker to audience or of speaker to content, while figures of language (Greek *skhêmata lekseos*, Latin *figurae elocutionis*) are understood as artistic patterns of words and sounds. Tropes replace normal language with unexpected words that nonetheless, due to context, make the meaning richer and/or clearer. What the speaker intends is different from the literal meaning of the trope. Tropes may thus be analyzed as figures of thought, or figures of language, or a category unto themselves.

Sample *figures of thought* include:

apostrophe   Address to an absent person or god.

dubitatio   (Greek *aporia*) Intentional expression of uncertainty or confusion on the part of the speaker.

hyperbole   Deliberate overstatement.

interrogatio (Greek *erôtêma*) Rhetorical question.

subiectio   (Greek *hypophora*) Mock dialogue.

oxymoron   Linking of seemingly contradictory terms.

sermocinatio (Greek *prosôpopoeia*) Speaking in the character of another person.

sententia   (Greek *gnômê*) A general idea formulated in a single, concise sentence.

praeteritio   (Greek *paraleipsis*) Mentioning things a speaker will leave out of the discussion so as to call more attention to them.

Sample *figures of language* include:

anaphora   Repetition of a word at the beginning of successive sentences or phrases.

epiphora   Repetition of a word at the end of successive sentences or phrases.

polyptoton   Repetition of the same word with different case endings (both Greek and Latin are highly inflected languages).

asyndeton   Omission of conjunctions where ordinarily expected.

polysyndeton Repetition of conjunctions to a greater extent than necessary.

hyperbaton   Placement of a word far from its normal position in a phrase or sentence.

isocolon   Construction of successive phrases or cola of the same length.

Sample *tropes* include:

metaphor   As in English, an implied comparison; substitution of a word or phrase from another semantic realm.

metonymy   Replacement of a word or group of words by another that has some relationship of meaning to the word replaced.

synecdoche   Replacement of a word by a word that refers to a part of the object described.

antonomosia   Periphrasis for a proper name.

litotes   Deliberate understatement.

hyperbole   Deliberate overstatement.

ironia   Irony, as in English.

Notes

Preface

1 Friedrich Nietzsche, "Description of Ancient Rhetoric," in *Friedrich Nietzsche on Rhetoric and Language*, edited and translated with a critical introduction by S. L. Gilman, C. Blair, and D. J. Parent (Oxford: Oxford University Press, 1989), pp. 3–194 (quotation from p. 3).

Chapter 1 Rhetoric and the State

1 Translation from the Greek as in V. Farenga, "Periphrasis on the Origin of Rhetoric," *Modern Language Notes* 94 (1979), pp. 1033–55 (translation on p. 1036).

Chapter 2 The Figure of the Orator

1 Quintilian, *Institutes* 11.1.39.
2 R. Syme, *Fictional History Old and New: Hadrian* (Oxford: Somerville College, 1986), a James Bryce Memorial Lecture delivered in the Wolfson Hall, Somerville College on May 10, 1984.

Chapter 3 The Craft of Rhetoric

1 See G. R. F. Ferrari, *Listening to the Cicadas: A Study of Plato's Phaedrus* (Cambridge: Cambridge University Press, 1987), esp. pp. 225–9.
2 M. Helms, *Craft and the Kingly Ideal* (Austin: University of Texas Press, 1993), p. 5.

3   Quotations from Aelius Aristides are taken from the translation of
    C. Behr: *P. Aelius Aristides, The Complete Works*, 2 vols. (Leiden: E. J. Brill,
    1981).
4   Ibid.

Chapter 4 Rhetoric as Acculturation

1   The phrase is that of R. Rappaport, *Ritual and Religion in the Making of
    Humanity* (Cambridge: Cambridge University Press), p. 322.

Chapter 5 The Afterlife of Rhetoric

1   G. Kennedy, *Classical Rhetoric and its Christian and Secular Tradition
    from Ancient to Modern Times* (Chapel Hill: University of North Carolina
    Press, 1980), p. 145.
2   J. Murphy, "One Thousand Neglected Authors: The Scope and Import-
    ance of Renaissance Rhetoric" in *Renaissance Eloquence*, ed. J. Murphy
    (Berkeley: University of California Press, 1983).
3   For use of the terms "electrify" and "abuse" with respect to revolutionary
    rhetoric, see A. Principato, "L'éloquence révolutionnaire: idéologie et
    légende," in *Histoire de la rhétorique dans l'Europe moderne, 1450–
    1950*, ed. M. Fumaroli (Paris: Presses Universitaires de France, 1999),
    pp. 1019–37.
4   T. Sprat, from *The History of the Royal-Society of London for the Improving
    of Natural Knowledge* (1667), as quoted in *The Rhetorical Tradition:
    Readings from Classical Times to the Present*, ed. P. Bizzell and
    B. Herzberg (Boston, MA: Bedford Books, 1990), p. 642.
5   S. Toulmin, from *The Uses of Argument*, as quoted in Bizzell and
    Herzberg, *The Rhetorical Tradition*, p. 1122.
6   Friedrich Nietzsche, "Description of Ancient Rhetoric," in *Friedrich
    Nietzsche on Rhetoric and Language*, edited and translated with a critical
    introduction by S. L. Gilman, C. Blair, and D. J. Parent (Oxford:
    Oxford University Press, 1989), p. 21.
7   F. Nietzsche, "On Truth and Lying in an Extra-Moral Sense," in *Friedrich
    Nietzsche on Rhetoric and Language*, edited with a critical introduction
    by S. L. Gilman, C. Blair, and D. J. Parent (Oxford: Oxford University
    Press, 1989), pp. 246–57 (quotation from p. 246).
8   Ibid, p. 248.
9   Ibid, p. 250.
10 Ibid, p. 248.
11 Ibid, p. 3.

12   P. Baehr, *Caesar and the Fading of the Roman World: A Study in Republicanism and Caesarism* (New Brunswick, NJ: Transaction Publishers, 1998).

13   H. White, "The Suppression of Rhetoric in the Nineteenth Century," in *The Rhetoric Canon*, edited by B. D. Schildgen (Detroit: Wayne State University Press, 1997), pp. 21–32 (quotation from p. 31).

14   B. McComiskey, *Gorgias and the New Sophistic Rhetoric* (Carbondale: Southern Illinois University Press, 2002), p. 117.

15   Ibid, p. 67.

16   K. Löwith, quoted in H.-H. Kögler, *The Power of Dialogue: Critical Hermeneutics after Gadamer and Foucault*, translated by P. Hendrickson (Cambridge, MA: MIT Press, 1996), p. 288, n. 14.

Further Reading

Primary Sources and General Background

Translations of most of the primary works discussed in this book can be found in the collection entitled Loeb Classical Library, published by Harvard University Press (Cambridge, MA). For the Greek orators, a new series of translations and commentaries, entitled *The Oratory of Classical Greece*, has recently begun to appear with the University of Texas Press (Austin) under the general editorship of M. Gagarin. For Thucydides, highly recommended is the translation by S. Lattimore: *The History of the Peloponnesian War* (Indianapolis, IN: Hackett, 1998). Aristotle's *Rhetoric* is probably best consulted in the translation and edition by George A. Kennedy, entitled *Aristotle On Rhetoric: A Theory of Civic Discourse* (Oxford: Oxford University Press, 1991). For Hermogenes, see M. Heath, *Hermogenes On Issues: Strategies of Argument in Later Greek Rhetoric* (Oxford: Oxford University Press, 1995) and C. Wooten, *Hermogenes' On Types of Style* (Chapel Hill: University of North Carolina Press, 1987), both of which are very helpful in clarifying an otherwise difficult writer. For Aelius Aristides consult the translation of *The Complete Works* by C. Behr (Leiden: Brill, 1981, 2 vols.), which also contains a useful commentary. Translations of selected examples of Greek political oratory and of the writings of Cicero, as well as individual treatises by Plato, can also be found in the Penguin Classics series (London). The fragmentary writings of the sophists are easily accessible in a collection entitled *The Older Sophists*, ed. R. K. Sprague (Indianapolis, IN: Hackett, 1972). For later Latin panegyric orations see E. Nixon and B. Rodgers, *In Praise of Later Roman Emperors* (Berkeley: University of California Press, 1994). For St. Augustine, *On Christian Doctrine*, see, in addition to the Loeb, the translation by D. W. Robertson (New York: Liberal Arts Press, 1958). An anthology entitled *The Rhetorical Tradition: Readings from Classical Times to the Present*, ed. P. Bizzell and B. Herzberg (Boston, MA: Bedford, 1990) contains a

good selection of material from ancient rhetorical treatises, but virtually no
oratory.

Earlier secondary works that provide a comprehensive overview of some
or all aspects of ancient rhetoric and oratory treated in this book include
G. Kennedy, *A New History of Classical Rhetoric* (Princeton, NJ: Princeton
University Press, 1994); S. Usher, *Greek Oratory: Tradition and Originality*
(Oxford: Oxford University Press, 1999); *Roman Eloquence: Rhetoric in
Society and Literature*, ed. W. Dominik (New York: Routledge, 1997);
J. Walker, *Rhetoric and Poetics in Antiquity* (Oxford: Oxford University
Press, 2000); and *The Orator in Action and Theory in Greece and Rome*, ed.
C. Wooten (Boston, MA: Brill, 2001).

Rhetoric and the State

On the emergence of the city-state in the Greek world there is a useful
collection of essays, *The Development of the Polis in Archaic Greece*, ed. L. G.
Mitchell and P. J. Rhodes (New York: Routledge, 1997). Also important
is Christian Meier, *The Greek Discovery of Politics*, trans. D. McClintock
(Cambridge, MA: Harvard University Press, 1990). Meier is concerned with
both structural and ideological aspects of state formation. On the Roman
side, I know of no single collection or monograph comparable to these two
works, but the essays in *Cambridge Ancient History, Vol. 7: The Rise of Rome
to 220 BC* (Cambridge: Cambridge University Press, 1989) address similar
issues. Also relevant are A. Grandazzi, *The Foundation of Rome: Myth and
History*, trans. J. M. Todd (Ithaca, NY: Cornell University Press, 1997) – a
wonderful combination of historical synthesis with reflection on the meaning
of "foundation"; *Social Struggles in Archaic Rome*, ed. K. Raaflaub (Berkeley:
University of California Press, 1986); and a short essay by C. Smith, entitled
"Servius Tullius, Cleisthenes, and the Emergence of the Polis in Central
Italy" in Mitchell and Rhodes (see above), pp. 208–16. Despite their high
quality, none of these works gives sufficient attention to the role of special
speech in the formation of stable communities. For such an approach, works
by anthropologists who consider a wide range of human communities must
be consulted. Relevant here are E. Gellner, *Anthropology and Politics: Revolu-
tions in the Sacred Grove* (Oxford: Blackwell, 1995); R. Rappaport, *Ritual
and Religion in the Making of Humanity* (Cambridge: Cambridge Studies
in Cultural Anthropology, 110: 1999); *Political Language and Oratory in
Traditional Societies*, ed. M. Bloch (New York: Academic Press, 1975); and
J. Gil, *Metamorphoses of the Body*, trans. S. Muecke (Minneapolis: University
of Minnesota Press, 1998) – challenging, but immensely rewarding. Often
quoted, but in my view less satisfying than the works just cited, is S. Tambiah,
"The Magical Power of Words," *Man: Journal of the Royal Anthropological*

Institute 3 (1968): 175–208. G. Nagy, *Pindar's Homer: The Lyric Possession of an Epic Past* (Baltimore, MD: Johns Hopkins University Press, 1990) applies anthropological discussion of ritualized speech to the emergence of the Greek poetic tradition. My own forthcoming study, *The World of Roman Song*, makes a comparable effort with respect to Roman literary, musical, and artistic culture.

On the historical and structural relationship between oratory and feuding, see D. Cohen, *Law, Violence, and Society in Classical Athens* (Cambridge: Cambridge University Press, 1995) and S. Johnstone, *Disputes and Democracy: The Consequences of Litigation in Ancient Athens* (Austin: University of Texas Press, 1999). Also helpful (but hard to get) is A. Kelly, *Damaging Voice: Language of Aggression for the Athenian Trial* (Berkeley dissertation, 1994).

On oratory as a mode of legitimation, for the Greek world, see J. Ober, *Mass and Elite in Democratic Athens* (Princeton, NJ: Princeton University Press, 1989); for the Roman, T. Habinek, "Cicero and the Bandits" in *The Politics of Latin Literature* (Princeton, NJ: Princeton University Press, 1998).

On the ideological function of the figure of the tyrant in Greek culture, excellent discussions include two papers by V. Farenga: "Periphrasis on the Origin of Rhetoric," *Modern Language Notes* 94 (1979): 1033–55 (which considers in particular the episode of the invention of rhetoric by Korax) and "The Paradigmatic Tyrant: Greek Tragedy and the Ideology of the Proper," *Helios* 8 (1981): 1–32, as well as L. Kurke, *Coins, Bodies, Games, and Gold: The Politics of Meaning in Archaic Greece* (Princeton, NJ: Princeton University Press, 1999). The sources on tyranny are presented in chronological order in G. Giorgini, *La città e il tiranno* (Milan: Giuffre, 1993). Once again, comparable work is not available on the Roman side, where scholars are still inclined to take accounts of tyrannical emperors more or less at face value. For those who read French, M. Cazenave, *Les Empereurs fous* (Paris: Imago, 1981) is a bracing corrective. See also the subtle analysis of the figure of the tyrant in the writings of Seneca the Elder in E. Gunderson, *Declamation, Paternity, and Identity: Authority and the Rhetorical Self* (Cambridge: Cambridge University Press, 2003). On the simultaneous appropriation and exclusion of the rhetorical power of the female, see the classic essay by Ann L. T. Bergren, "Language and the Female in Early Greek Thought," *Arethusa* 16 (1983): 69–95. In my opinion, considerations of gender have still not been fully integrated into the study of the formation of ancient states. Historians take it as a given that the ancient state privileges males, and many (like Bergren) consider the ideological and other strategies through which male privilege is sustained. But why states should be bastions of male privilege – apart from a separation of labor between reproduction and fighting – is a question not given as much attention as it deserves.

For an overview of the specific political systems that emerged in Athens and Rome and formed the context for much of political oratory, see J. Ober, *The Athenian Revolution: Essays on Greek Democracy and Political Theory* (Princeton, NJ: Princeton University Press, 1995), as well as *Mass and Elite* (cited above); M. Crawford and M. Beard, *Rome in the Late Republic* (London: Duckworth, 1985); and in P. Jones and K. Sidwell, *The World of Rome: An Introduction to Roman Culture* (Cambridge: Cambridge University Press, 1997), chapter entitled "Governing Rome." On ancient Greek legal systems, helpful discussions include *Greek Law in its Political Setting: Justifications Not Justice*, ed. L. Foxhall and A. D. E. Lewis (Oxford: Clarendon Press, 1996) and D. Allen, *The World of Prometheus: The Politics of Punishing in Democratic Athens* (Princeton, NJ: Princeton University Press, 2000); for Rome, R. Baumann, *Crime and Punishment in Ancient Rome* (New York: Routledge, 1996) and A. Riggsby, *Crime and Community in Ciceronian Rome* (Austin: University of Texas Press, 1999). On display oratory (i.e., epideictic), especially in the Greek cities under the Roman empire, there is a lively account in M. Gleason, *Making Men: Sophists and Self-Presentation in Ancient Rome* (Princeton, NJ: Princeton University Press, 1995). For oratory at the end of the classical period, see D. A. Russell, *Greek Declamation* (Cambridge: Cambridge University Press, 1983) and the first chapter of S. MacCormack, *Art and Ceremony in Late Antiquity* (Berkeley: University of California Press, 1981).

The Figure of the Orator

I know of no single study that examines the heroization of the orator as a cross-cultural phenomenon in ancient or modern times. Still important for understanding how different models of leadership develop in different social contexts is M. Weber, *Economy and Society*, 2 vols., ed. G. Roth and C. Wittich (Berkeley: University of California Press, 1978) and "Politics as a Vocation," in *From Max Weber*, ed. and trans. H. H. Gerth and C. Wright Mills (London: Routledge and Kegan Paul, 1970), pp. 77–128.

Biographies of the orators discussed in this chapter abound, but they tend to overemphasize the almost impossible task of sorting fact from fiction, rather than understanding the social and cultural significance of the figure of the orator. Still, R. Sealey, *Demosthenes and His Time* (Oxford: Oxford University Press, 1993) and T. Mitchell, *Cicero: The Ascending Years* (New Haven, CT: Yale University Press, 1979) and *Cicero: The Senior Statesman* (New Haven, CT: Yale University Press, 1991) provide much useful information, as does the collection of essays entitled *Demosthenes: Statesman and Orator*, ed. I. Worthington (New York: Routledge, 2000). A new book by J. Dugan, *Making a New Man: Ciceronian Self-Fashioning*

(Oxford: Oxford University Press, 2004) shows how Cicero uses discourse, both oral and written, to project an image independent of his non-aristocratic background. The impact of that image on successive generations of Romans remains to be studied, although an old German work, T. Zielinski, *Cicero im Wandel der Jahrhundert* (Leipzig: Teubner, 1912) provides the raw material. My own study, "Seneca's Renown: *Gloria, Claritudo*, and the Replication of the Roman Elite," *Classical Antiquity* 19 (2000): 264–303, examines how the philosopher and orator Seneca the Younger came to be regarded as a cultural exemplar whose success (like Cicero's) through control of discourse legitimized new processes of social mobility under the Roman empire. In general my approach in this chapter is indebted to V. Wohl, *Love Among the Ruins: The Erotics of Democracy in Classical Athens* (Princeton, NJ: Princeton University Press, 2002). Wohl carefully analyzes the language of fifth and fourth-century BC Athenian texts to explore the political unconscious as made manifest in depictions of Pericles, Creon, Alcibiades, and others.

Other works of interest on particular topics touched upon in this chapter include N. Loraux, *The Invention of Athens*, trans. A. Sheridan (Cambridge, MA: Harvard University Press, 1986), a classic study of the role of funeral oration in the formation of Athenian identity; R. Morstein-Marx, *Mass Oratory and Political Power in the Late Roman Republic* (Cambridge: Cambridge University Press, 2004); and, for those who read French, the magisterial study of J.-M. David, *Le Patronat judiciaire au dernier siècle de la république romaine* (Rome: Ecole française de Rome, 1992), which considers the relationship among orator, client, jury, and audience at Rome from a variety of perspectives. A short essay by B. Dufallo, entitled "Appius' Indignation: Gossip, Tradition, and Performance in Republican Rome," *Transactions and Proceedings of the American Philological Association* 131 (2001): 119–42, offers an insightful analysis of Cicero's evocation of the dead in his speech "In Defense of Caelius." My understanding of the social dynamics underlying Cicero's speech "In Defense of Cluentius" has been greatly assisted by student seminar presentations some years ago by Sarah Morrison and P. Isaac Miller. To my knowledge, neither has been published.

The Craft of Rhetoric

Two important books – T. Cole, *The Origins of Rhetoric in Ancient Greece* (Baltimore, MD: Johns Hopkins University Press, 1991) and E. Schiappa, *The Beginnings of Rhetorical Theory in Classical Greece* (New Haven, CT: Yale University Press, 1999) – place the development of rhetoric as a distinct field of study in the fourth century BC. While they do not emphasize the point, their analysis suggests that the circumscription of rhetoric was an attempt by Plato and his contemporaries to subordinate it to the newly emergent co-discipline of philosophy. In the generation prior to Plato a group of thinkers whom he rather dismissively identified as sophists taught speechmaking and reflected deeply on the relationship between language and reality and on the social function of formalized language. Their activity is the subject of two outstanding scholarly works by J. de Romilly: *Magic and Rhetoric in Ancient Greece* (Cambridge, MA: Harvard University Press, 1975) and *The Great Sophists of Periclean Athens*, trans. J. Lloyd (Oxford: Clarendon Press, 1992). In line with de Romilly's approach, other scholars have begun to reassess the sophists as prototypes of contemporary approaches to language, politics, and subject formation: see, for example, S. Jarratt, *Rereading the Sophists* (Carbondale: Southern Illinois University Press, 1991, 1998); S. Consigny, *Gorgias: Sophist and Artist* (Columbia: University of South Carolina Press, 2001); and B. McComiskey, *Gorgias and the New Sophistic Rhetoric* (Carbondale: Southern Illinois University Press, 2002). As indicated in the text, my own interpretation of the craft metaphor that runs throughout ancient discussions of rhetoric has been strongly influenced by M. Helms, *Craft and the Kingly Ideal: Art, Trade, and Power* (Austin: University of Texas Press, 1993).

Scholarly investigation of the individual handbooks and speeches discussed in this chapter has intensified in recent years, although not all works have received equal attention. For example, there is no comprehensive study of the intellectual or cultural significance of Lysias' speeches despite extensive work on questions of authenticity and value as source material for the study of history. Plato's approach to rhetoric – and, incidentally, to the figure of Lysias – receives thoughtful consideration in G. Ferrari, *Listening to the Cicadas: A Study of Plato's Phaedrus* (Cambridge: Cambridge University Press, 1987). In general, scholarship on Plato still absorbs and perpetuates the Athenian philosopher's anti-rhetorical bias, an exception being A. Nightingale, *Genres in Dialogue: Plato and the Construct of Philosophy* (Cambridge: Cambridge University Press, 1995), which rightly treats the emergence of philosophy as itself a contingent and interested historical process. H. Yunis, *Taming Democracy: Models of Political Rhetoric in Classical Democracy* (Ithaca, NY: Cornell University Press, 1996), makes the case that in the *Laws*, a product of his later years, Plato found a way of reconciling his foundationalist epistemology with the political and social claims of rhetoric.

For Aristotle's *Rhetoric*, as indicated above, there is now a good translation with much guidance through a chaotic text by G. A. Kennedy: *Aristotle On Rhetoric: A Theory of Civic Discourse* (Oxford: Oxford University Press, 1991). The essays in A. O. Rorty, *Essays on Aristotle's Rhetoric* (Berkeley: University of California Press, 1996) situate the *Rhetoric* as part of Aristotle's larger philosophical project, but offer little in the way of serious critical evaluation of Aristotle's contribution to the field of rhetoric. Here too the relative prestige accorded to philosophy in the modern academy has left its mark. The *Rhetorica ad Herennium* is still best consulted in the Loeb edition (facing Latin and English) of H. Caplan, with helpful notes. Pliny's *Panegyricus* is available in the Loeb Classical Library series: for discussion, see S. Bartsch, *Actors in the Audience: Theatricality and Doublespeak from Nero to Hadrian* (Cambridge, MA: Harvard University Press, 1994). On the social role of imperial panegyric, as on many other topics considered in this chapter, a great deal of creative, sympathetic work remains to be done.

Finally, a number of efforts have been made to systematize ancient rhetoric, that is to write summary accounts based on teachings shared across and among generations of handbooks in Greek and Latin. The most important of these compendia is H. Lausberg, *Handbook of Literary Rhetoric* (Leiden: Brill, 1998). As indicated in the text, Lausberg deliberately omits consideration of memory and performance, but his discussion of invention and style, while tough going, is illuminating, even for the expert. Lausberg made his career teaching medieval and modern French literature and he developed his handbook primarily as an aid to those interested in the impact of classical rhetoric on later literature. But his encyclopedic knowledge of the ancient sources and accurate interpretation of individual passages make his work indispensable even for those whose focus is on the social function of rhetoric in classical antiquity. For what it's worth, the German original of Lausberg's study, which I encountered in graduate school a quarter of a century ago, was the work that first got me thinking seriously about ancient rhetoric as a field of inquiry. Also helpful, if more modest in scope, are P. Corbett, *Classical Rhetoric for the Modern Student* (Oxford: Oxford University Press, 1990) and R. Lanham, *A Handlist of Rhetorical Terms* (Berkeley: University of California Press, 1991).

Rhetoric as Acculturation

Study of ancient education and of the relationship between dominant and subordinate cultures in the ancient world is very much in ferment. For a political and social perspective on interaction between cultures, especially in the later Roman empire, see C. Ando, *Imperial Ideology and Provincial Loyalty in the Roman Empire* (Berkeley: University of California Press, 2000). T. Whitmarsh, *Greek Literature and the Roman Empire: The Politics of Imitation* (Oxford: Oxford University Press, 2001), considers issues of cultural continuity and transformation as manifest in literary texts. On the meaning and social significance of Hellenism, especially in the East, the writings of G. Bowersock are indispensable: see in particular his *Hellenism in Late Antiquity* (Ann Arbor: University of Michigan Press, 1990). Just as political history has reconsidered the agency of provincials, so educational history has begun to pay closer attention to activities outside the great centers of Rome and Athens. For a traditional account of Greek and Roman education, the standard work is H.-I. Marrou, *A History of Education in Antiquity*, trans. G. Lamb (Madison: University of Wisconsin Press, 1982 and New York: Sheed and Ward, 1956). S. Bonner, *Education in Ancient Rome* (Berkeley: University of California Press, 1977), is plodding but informative. More stimulating is R. Cribiore, *Gymnastics of the Mind: Greek Education in Hellenistic and Roman Egypt* (Princeton, NJ: Princeton University Press, 2001). Despite the geographical limitation suggested by the title, Cribiore in fact does an excellent job of putting education in Egypt – for which there is extensive papyrological evidence – in the broader context of literary and rhetorical education throughout the ancient world. R. Kaster, *Guardians of Language: The Grammarian and Society and Late Antiquity* (Berkeley: University of California Press, 1988), provides a useful account of the educational projects and social status of the grammatici, whose work preceded that of the rhetores in the usual education sequence.

Several works by W. M. Bloomer – "Schooling in Persona: Imagination and Subordination in Roman Education," *Classical Antiquity* 16 (1997): 57–78; "A Preface to the History of Declamation: Whose Speech? Whose History?," in *The Roman Cultural Revolution*, ed. T. Habinek and A. Schiesaro (Cambridge: Cambridge University Press, 1997), pp. 199–215; and *Latinity and Literary Society at Rome* (Philadelphia: University of Pennsylvania Press, 1997) – explicitly consider ancient education as acculturation into elite status. This line of inquiry is shared especially by scholars who focus on the role of rhetorical education in the construction of masculine subjectivity. Examples of this approach include M. Gleason, *Making Men*, cited above under chapter 1; A. Richlin, "Gender and Rhetoric: Producing Manhood in the Schools," in *Roman Eloquence*, ed. W. Dominik (New York: Routledge, 1997), pp. 90–110; J. Connolly, "Mastering Corruption: Constructions of Identity in Roman Oratory," in *Women and Slaves in Greco-Roman Culture: Differential Equations*, ed. S. Joshel and S. Murnaghan (New York: Routledge, 1998), 130–51; and two books by E. Gunderson: *Staging Masculinity: The Rhetoric of Performance in the Roman World* (Ann Arbor: University of Michigan Press, 2000) and *Declamation, Paternity, and Identity: Authority and the Rhetorical Self* (Cambridge: Cambridge University Press, 2003). The politics of language use, especially in the Roman world, figures prominently in T. Habinek, *The Politics of Latin Literature* (Princeton, NJ: Princeton University Press, 1998) and, most recently, in J. N. Adams, "*Romanitas* and the Latin Language," in *Classical Quarterly* 53 (2003): 184–205. J. Waquet, *Latin, or the Empire of the Sign*, trans. J. Howe (London: Verso, 2000), considers the political and social role of Latin from the sixteenth through the twentieth centuries AD.

The Afterlife of Rhetoric

For a concise and insightful overview of the history of rhetoric in the Western tradition see R. Barilli, *Rhetoric*, trans. G. Menozzi (Minneapolis: University of Minneapolis Press, 1989). G. A. Kennedy, *Classical Rhetoric and its Christian and Secular Tradition from Ancient to Modern Times* (Chapel Hill: University of North Carolina Press, 1980), covers some of the same ground, but in more detail. Also very helpful are the introductory essays in Bizzell and Herzberg (cited under Primary Sources and General Studies, above). Read through in sequence they provide a coherent, analytical account of the history of rhetorical theory in the West. M. Fumaroli, *Histoire de la rhétorique dans l'Europe moderne, 1450–1950* (Paris: Presses Universitaires de France, 1999), is indispensable for the half millennium indicated in its title. All four works (although less so Fumaroli) focus on rhetoric as an academic discipline to the neglect of rhetoric and oratory as social practices with broad political and cultural consequences. The topic announced in *Rhetoric and Hermeneutics in Our Time: A Reader*, ed. W. Jost and M. Hyde (New Haven, CT: Yale University Press, 1997) is deliberately vague, even a bit misleading. In fact the collection contains a number of outstanding investigations of rhetoric, past and present, as a strategy for the production and interpretation of discourse.

Readers interested in learning more about Isocrates' role in the dissemination of rhetorical ideals will learn much from Y. Too, *The Rhetoric of Identity in Isocrates* (Cambridge: Cambridge University Press, 1995) and T. Poulakos, *Speaking for the Polis: Isocrates' Rhetorical Education* (Columbia: University of South Carolina Press, 1997). The argument of H. Yunis, *Taming Democracy: Models of Political Rhetoric in Classical Athens* (Ithaca, NY: Cornell University Press, 1996), although it concerns chiefly Thucydides and Plato, can usefully be put in dialogue with work on Isocrates. Yunis' account of Plato's accommodation with rhetoric later in his career by de-emphasizing public competition seems to dovetail with Isocrates' own legitimation of non-agonistic modes of rhetoric. The role of kairos in ancient thought – from Gorgias and Isocrates through the early Christians – is the focus of *Rhetoric and Kairos: Essays in History, Theory, and Praxis*, ed. P. Sipiora and J. Baumlin (Albany: State University of New York Press, 2002). Of related interest is J. Kinneavy, *Greek Rhetorical Origins of Christian Faith: An Inquiry* (Oxford: Oxford University Press, 1987), which addresses the connection between rhetorical and Christian notions of pistis.

For rhetoric in the early modern period, various essays in the collections listed above are helpful, perhaps especially V. Kahn, "Humanism and the Resistance to Theory," in Jost and Hyde, pp. 149–70, which considers, among other things "the democratization of learning in the form of easily accessible techniques" (p. 158). For the rhetoric of the French Revolution I have found helpful the paper by A. Principato, "L'éloquence révolutionnaire: idéologie et légende" in Fumaroli, pp. 1019–38. Nietzsche's writings on rhetoric are translated and analyzed in *Friedrich Nietzsche on Rhetoric and Language*, ed. S. Gilman, C. Blair, and D. Parent (Oxford: Oxford University Press, 1989). The key works of C. Perelman have been translated into English: they include C. Perelman and L. Olbrechts-Tyteca, *The New Rhetoric: A Treatise on Argumentation*, trans. J. Wilkinson and P. Weaver (Notre Dame, IN: University of Notre Dame Press, 1969) and C. Perelman, *The Realm of Rhetoric*, trans. W. Kluback (Notre Dame, IN: University of Notre Dame Press, 1982).

The key work of S. Toulmin referred to in the text is *The Uses of Argument* (Cambridge: Cambridge University Press, 1958; updated edition 2003). For a concise account of the work of Derrida (which is of course still very much in progress) see C. Norris, *Deconstruction: Theory and Practice* (New York: Routledge, 2003). Finally, books by Jarratt, McComiskey, and Consigny (cited under chapter 3 above), as well as several of the papers in Jost and Hyde, might be seen as representative of the reclamation of ancient rhetoric for contemporary democratic projects; so, too, an excellent forthcoming study by political theorist Danielle Allen, entitled *Talking to Strangers: Little Rock and Political Friendship* (Chicago: University of Chicago Press, 2004). Allen emphasizes the role of rhetoric in creating conditions of trust that make democratic citizenship possible. Her analysis focuses on recent American political discourse, but looks back to the classical tradition as well. My own conception of democracy as a means of "recomposing the world" is based on A. Touraine, *What is Democracy?*, trans. D. Macey (Boulder, CO: Westview Press, 1997). Touraine is especially interested in developing a concept and practice of democratic culture that would not be limited to a narrowly institutional framework. On this approach, which a revival of rhetoric would strongly support, see also the writings of anti-foundationalist political theorists such as B. Barber, "Foundationalism and Democracy" in *Democracy and Difference: Contesting the Boundaries of the Political,* ed. S. Benhabib (Princeton, NJ: Princeton University Press, 1996), pp. 348–60.

Annotated Index

Names and terms that may be unfamiliar or that are used in a technical sense are supplied with a brief identification in parentheses.

Academy (ancient school of philosophy, founded by Plato), 80

acculturation, 61–2, 67–8, 81, 89, 118

Acropolis (citadel of Athens), 14

actio (Latin: performance), 65

actors, 102

adultery (declamatory theme), 105

Aelius Aristides (Publius Aelius Aristides, Greek sophist, second century AD), 45, 56–9

Afghanistan, 62

Agamemnon (character in Petronius, *Satyricon*), 85

Alcibiades (Athenian orator and general, fifth century BC), 23–5, 115

Alexander the Great (Alexander III of Macedon, general, fourth century BC), 16, 20, 46, 62, 75

Alexandria, 60, 64

Allen, Danielle, 99, 120

alliteration, 56

ambiguity (one of the stances), 104

Americas, 91

anadiplosis (figure of language in which word at end of a unit is repeated at beginning of subsequent unit), 46

anaphora (figure of language in which same word is repeated at beginning of successive phrases), 56, 106

anthropology, 4–6, 33, 52–4, 112–13

antilogy (structured argument on both sides of a question), 73

Antioch, 60, 76

antithesis, 21

Antoninus Pius (Roman emperor, second century AD), 58

Antonius (Marcus Antonius, Roman orator and politician, second and first century BC, character in Cicero, *De Oratore*), 73

antonomasia (trope: periphrasis for proper name), 107

Antony (Marcus Antonius, "Mark Antony," Roman orator and general, first century BC), 8, 11, 77

apomnemoneusis (Greek: remembering), 41

aporia (figure of thought: feigned uncertainty), 106

aposiopesis (figure of thought: self-imposed interruption), 55

erotema (Greek: figure of language
   consisting of rhetorical question),
   106
ethics, 17, 72, 75
ethnicity, 15, 87
ethos (mode of persuasion relying on
   character), 21–2, 42–3, 48, 51,
   103
eulogy, 36, 53–4; *see also* praise,
   speeches of
Euripides (Athenian tragedian, fifth
   century BC), 85
excitatio (Latin: summoning of the
   dead), 30–1; *see also* conjuring
exclusiveness of rhetoric, vii, 2–7, 42,
   53, 63–5
exempla (examples), 28, 36, 45–6,
   75
exhortation, vii, 57

faith, Christian, 87–8
fathers and sons (declamatory theme),
   70–1, 77–8
feudalism, 91
feuding, 3, 113
fides (Latin: believability, belief), 88
figurae elocutionis (Latin: figures of
   language), 105
figurae sententiae (Latin: figures of
   thought), 105
figuration, 97–8
figures of language (= figures of
   speech), 50, 105–6
figures of thought, 50, 105–6
forensic (Latin forense: type of
   oratory concerning judicial
   matters), 3, 85, 103
formalization, 5–6
forum, Roman, 14, 46, 79
Foucault, Michel, 96
France, 90, 95
freedom of speech, 7, 76; *see also*
   libertas
French language, 64
French Revolution, 91–2
funerals, 17–19, 36–7, 54, 58, 76,
   115

Gaul, 52, 61, 62
Gaza, 76
Gellius (Aulus Gellius, Roman writer,
   second century AD), 66
Gelon (tyrant of Syracuse, fifth
   century BC), 9, 11
gender, 62, 66, 113; *see also* male
   privilege; manliness; women
gesture, 4, 65–6, 102
Getic language, 63
globalism, 76, 99
glory, 35–6, 57
gnome (Greek: figure of thought
   entailing concise expression of
   complex idea), 106
goals of rhetoric, classical formulation
   of, 47
God (Judaeo-Christian), 86–7
Gorgias (Greek teacher, speaker, and
   thinker; a sophist; fifth century
   AD), 39, 41, 65, 80, 86, 97, 119
Gospel of John, 86–7
Gracchus (Gaius Sempronius
   Gracchus, Roman politician and
   orator, second century BC), 30
grammaticus (teacher of language and
   literature; pl. grammatici), 60,
   74, 118
gratia (Latin term for political loyalty,
   gratitude for favors done), 25
Greek language, 62–5
Gregory of Nazianzus (Christian
   bishop and orator, fourth century
   AD), 88
grooming, 102

Habermas, Jürgen, 98
Hadrian (Publius Aelius Hadrianus,
   Roman emperor, second century
   AD), 37, 64
handbooks (treatises), 41, 43–52,
   56–7, 64, 75
Hebrew, 86
hegemony, 63, 75, 77
Heidegger, Martin, 96
Hellenism, 75–6, 78, 117
Helms, Mary, 52–3